CW00349554

PRESENTED BY

EST. MMXI

LIQUID HISTORY

—— TOURS ——

Drunk on history since 2011, Liquid History Tours
run London's leading pub tours. After walking
100,000 miles, and sinking over 200,000 pints,
this is our hand-picked selection of over 50 pubs
you should visit at least once in your life.

Cheers !

John

LIQUID
HISTORY

An Illustrated Guide to
London's Greatest Pubs

John Warland

BANTAM PRESS

TRANSWORLD PUBLISHERS

Penguin Random House, One Embassy Gardens, 8 Viaduct Gardens, London SW I I 7BW

www.penguin.co.uk

Transworld is part of the Penguin Random House group of companies
whose addresses can be found at global.penguinrandomhouse.com

First published in Great Britain in 202 I by Bantam Press
an imprint of Transworld Publishers

Illustrations: Emma Majury
Design concept and maps: Pearlfisher

A CIP catalogue record for this book
is available from the British Library.

ISBN 9781787634893

Typeset in Johnston ITC Std 8.5/11.5pt
Printed and bound in Great Britain by Clays Ltd, Elcograf S.p.A.

The authorised representative in the EEA is Penguin Random House Ireland,
Morrison Chambers, 32 Nassau Street, Dublin D02 YH68.

Penguin Random House is committed to a sustainable
future for our business, our readers and our planet. This book
is made from Forest Stewardship Council® certified paper.

An Englishman, an Irishman
and a Scotsman walk into a bar.

The barman looks up and says,
'Is this some kind of joke?'

To Cc x

CONTENTS

The Lamb (p. 20)

The Queens Larder (p. 85)

Bloomsbury

Holborn Whippet (p. 149)

Cittie of Yorke (p. 105)

Ye Olde Mitre (p. 61)

Princess Louise (p. 96)

The Ship Tavern (p. 80)

The Seven Stars (p. 73)

The Tipperary (p. 132)

The Cross Keys (p. 125)

Ye Olde Cheshire Cheese (p. 12)

Ye Olde Cock Tavern (p. 112)

The Old Bell Tavern (p. 115)

The Coach & Horses (p. 31)

The French House (p. 26)

The George (p. 168)

Lamb & Flag (p. 25)

Mooney's (p. 188)

The Harp (p. 147)

The Coal Hole (p. 167)

The Nell Gwynne (p. 64)

The Ship & Shovell (p. 101)

CLOSE AT HAND

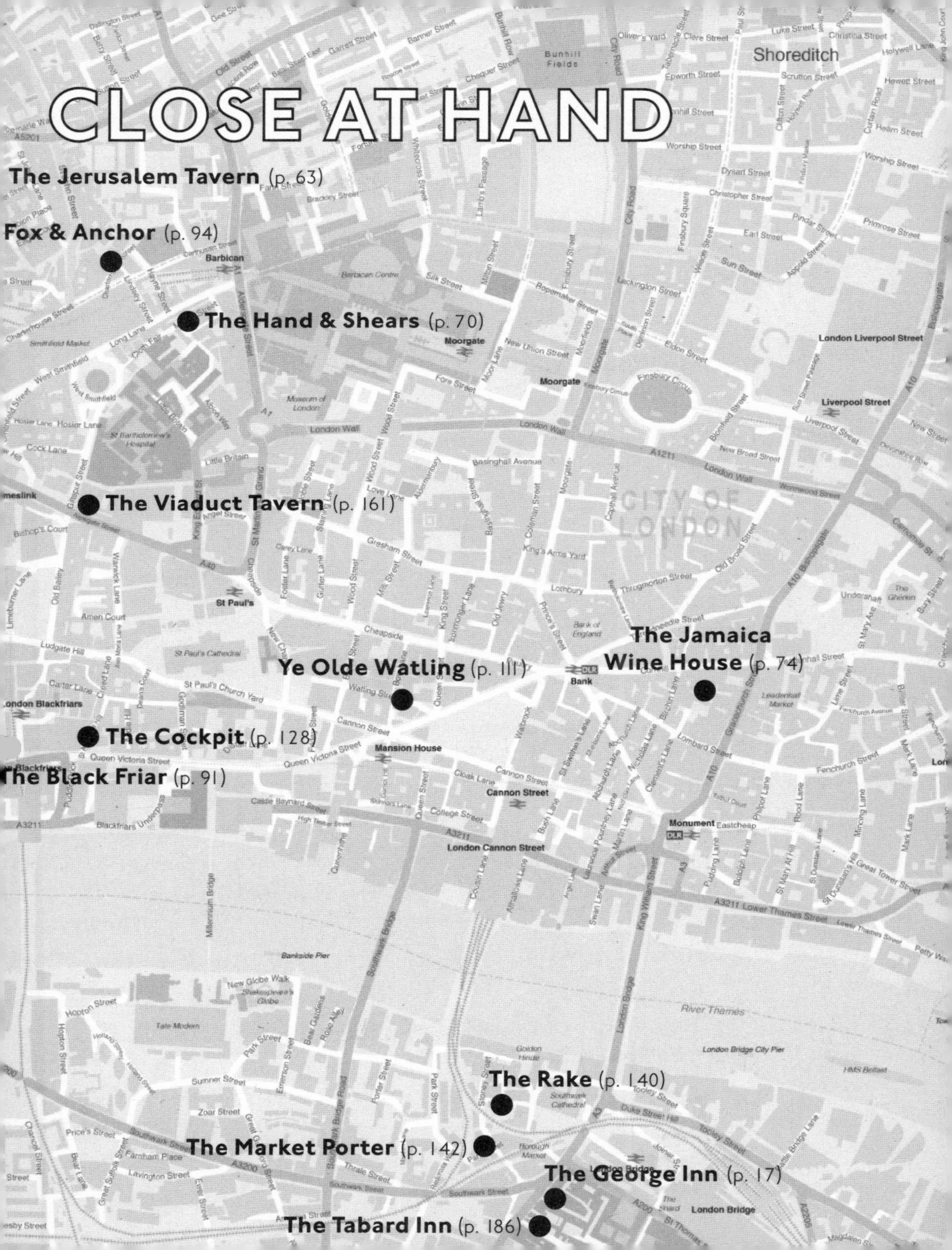
The Jerusalem Tavern (p. 63)
Fox & Anchor (p. 94)
The Hand & Shears (p. 70)
The Viaduct Tavern (p. 161)
The Jamaica Wine House (p. 74)
Ye Olde Watling (p. 111)
The Cockpit (p. 128)
The Black Friar (p. 91)
The Rake (p. 140)
The Market Porter (p. 142)
The George Inn (p. 17)
The Tabard Inn (p. 186)
Shoreditch
Bunhill Fields
Barbican
Moorgate
London Liverpool Street
Liverpool Street
St Paul's
Bank
Mansion House
Cannon Street
London Cannon Street
Monument
London Bridge
City of London
River Thames

The Spaniards Inn (p. 22)

The Holly Bush (p. 82)

The Magdala (p. 171)

Crocker's Folly (p. 185)

Euston Tap (p. 14

The Prince Alfred (p. 108)

The Fitzroy Tavern (p. 28

The Wheatsheaf (p. 32)

Star & Garter (p. 122)

The Guinea (Grill) (p. 78)

The Lyric (p. 1

The Churchill Arms (p. 102)

The Red Lion (p. 77)

The Grenadier (p. 66)

The Nags Head (p. 69)

The Star Tavern
(p. 163)

The Dove(s) (p. 39)

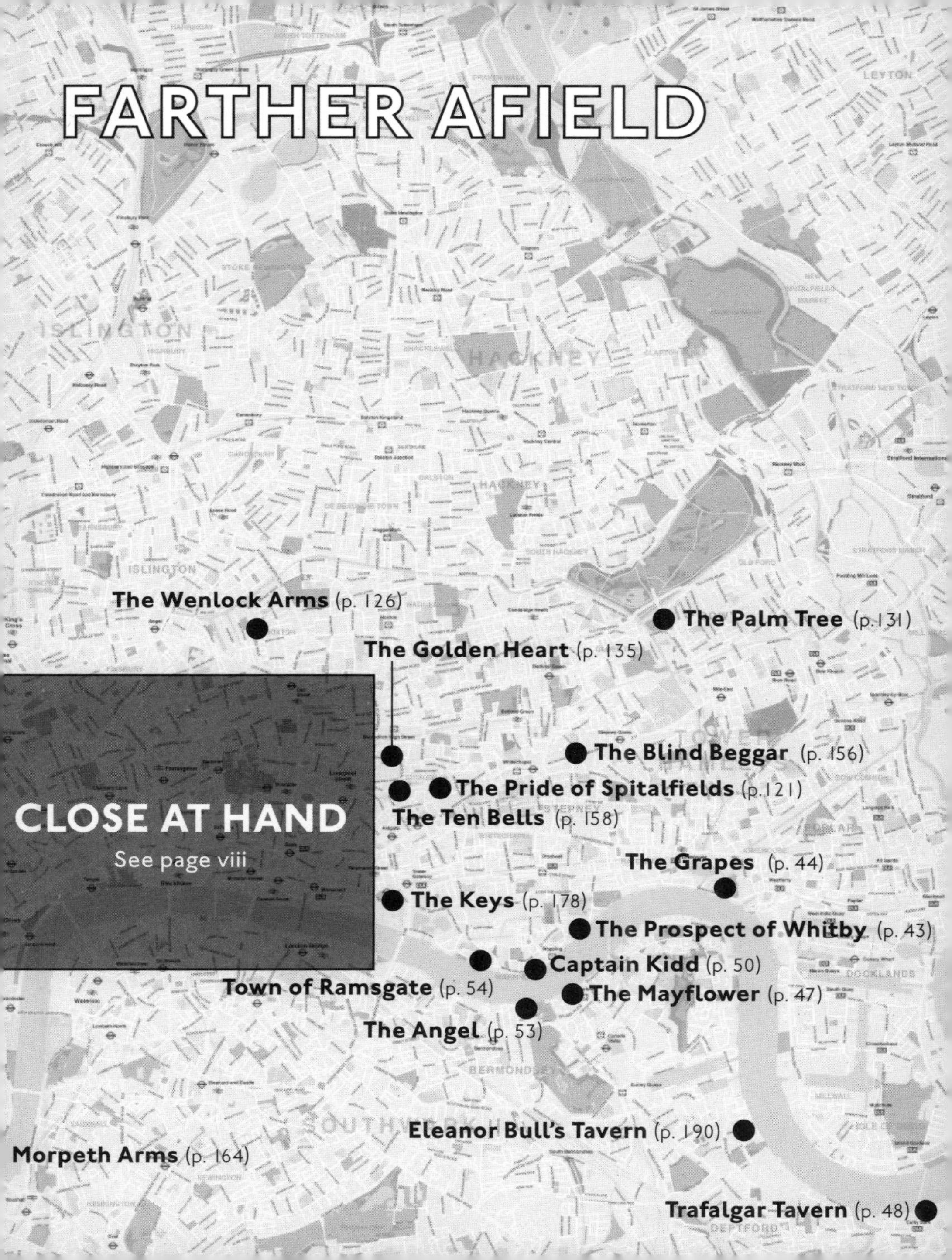

FARTHER AFIELD
The Wenlock Arms (p. 126)
The Palm Tree (p.131)
The Golden Heart (p. 135)
The Blind Beggar (p. 156)
The Pride of Spitalfields (p.121)
CLOSE AT HAND
See page viii
The Ten Bells (p. 158)
The Grapes (p. 44)
The Keys (p. 178)
The Prospect of Whitby (p. 43)
Captain Kidd (p. 50)
Town of Ramsgate (p. 54)
The Mayflower (p. 47)
The Angel (p. 53)
Eleanor Bull's Tavern (p. 190)
Morpeth Arms (p. 164)
Trafalgar Tavern (p. 48)
ISLINGTON
HACKNEY
BERMONDSEY
DOCKLANDS
LEYTON
DEPTFORD

pub:

(*puhb*) **Noun**

(Formal) **Public House**

1. A meeting place where people attempt to achieve advanced states of mental incompetence by the repeated consumption of fermented vegetable drinks – Kryten, *Red Dwarf*

See also: inn, tavern, alehouse, boozer, battlecruiser, rub-a-dub, watering hole

THE LONDON PUB

FOREWORD by Dan Cruickshank

LONDON'S PUBS REMAIN ONE of the city's great architectural glories and wonders of convivial life. The last two decades have taken a tough toll. Many fine pubs have closed but – as this invaluable guide makes clear – the London pub is still very much alive. However, if we want to keep our pubs they have to be fought for and this inspiring ode to some of London's best pubs will surely aid and bolster those determined to save buildings that – in many ways – represent the heart and soul of the city.

Pubs close for many reasons and sometimes it is an insidious business, with the victims being converted from primarily public houses to primarily restaurants. But these, of course, are two very different things.

From the start of its long history – stretching back to the inns of the Middle Ages and the taverns of the 18th century – the London pub has offered food and, on occasion, accommodation, but its main purpose has been to offer its customers alcohol – ale, beer, spirits, wine or even cider – served in pleasant, comfortable, inspiring or fantastic settings. The epitome of the London pub takes form in the 1870s when they become microcosms of the larger world, with public bars for the working man, saloon bars for the bosses (their bars masked by 'snob' screens that survive in the Lamb in Bloomsbury and the Prince Alfred in Little Venice), and snugs and private bars

for women, for more intimate conversation or for off-sales. Some of these later 19th-century pubs, with complex plans, etched glass, mirrors and flickering gaslights, were architectural jewels offering escapist fantasy. The Princess Louise in Holborn, called here 'the finest gin-palace-style pub still in existence', is a good example.

And it is the setting, of whatever character it might take, and the atmosphere that it evokes, that makes a public house distinct. The public house at its best is not merely a bar or restaurant, but a way of life: a place in which to immerse oneself, a place in which to enjoy life and to enjoy the company not only of friends but also of strangers. A truly great pub is a place where all manner of people – of different ages, backgrounds, trades or professions – meet, drink and commune. The moment you enter a real pub you know it. In the outer world you might be shocked if a stranger approaches you, but once past the pub's portal you welcome encounters, enjoy the pleasant cut and thrust of casual conversation, and feel liberated and intoxicated beyond the power of mere alcohol. There is so much to learn – not least tolerance and understanding – so when yet another good pub closes it is one more blow against a way of life and an institution that has done much and – as this book makes clear – continues to do much to make London the great city it is.

THE BEST JOB IN THE WORLD

INTRODUCTION

THE IDEA OF GETTING paid to go to the pub was of course conceived whilst drinking in one. The Black Dog in Vauxhall, if you're curious. Two guys, avoiding careers, convention and commutes, one pint at a time. The concept was simple – to share some of the greatest pubs from one of the world's greatest cities. To seek out the pubs that bear witness to London's history. The ones that survived plague, fire and war. And thus, Liquid History Tours was born. Offering 2,000 years of history, four pubs and plenty of elbow-bending activity rolled into a three-hour stroll for all to enjoy.

From Romans tippling in their taverns, to the glugging of weak ale and mead whilst Viking raids tore down London Bridge, the history of London's inhabitants is inextricably linked to that of its pubs. Our boozers are as much a part of the landscape and heritage as our hedgerows, the shipping forecast and rail replacement services. They are a place for monarchs and miscreants alike. Whether planning the Great Train Robbery, knocking off a gangland rival or signing off on the Communist Manifesto, the great London pub has really seen it all. They are an all-time purveyor of life's essentials including food, drink and camaraderie. So step inside, let your intoxicated mind wander, and allow the city's layers of liquid history to unfold before you.

As for the technicalities, an inn (with rooms for the night) might be an alehouse (purveyor of beer), but an alehouse isn't necessarily an inn. Both may be deemed pubs (short for public house), but neither is a tavern (purveyor of wine). It's all really quite simple once you've had a flagon or ten!

The catch-all term of 'pub' is a latterly adopted phrase used in contrast to the more elitist private members' clubs that had sprung up in the early 20th century. The more gentlemanly aspect of inns and taverns was slowly diluting at this time, whilst the good old class system was plain for all to see, in the use of public, saloon and snug divisions. *Plebeians . . . know your place!*

Unfortunately the traditional wine-serving taverns are now long gone, and coaching inns have fallen by the wayside due to the advent of the railways and motorised vehicles. The smell of manure has drifted away from the confines of inns and mews pubs, to be replaced only by a faint whiff of nostalgia.

Having a pint in a traditional London pub often still ranks at the top of many a

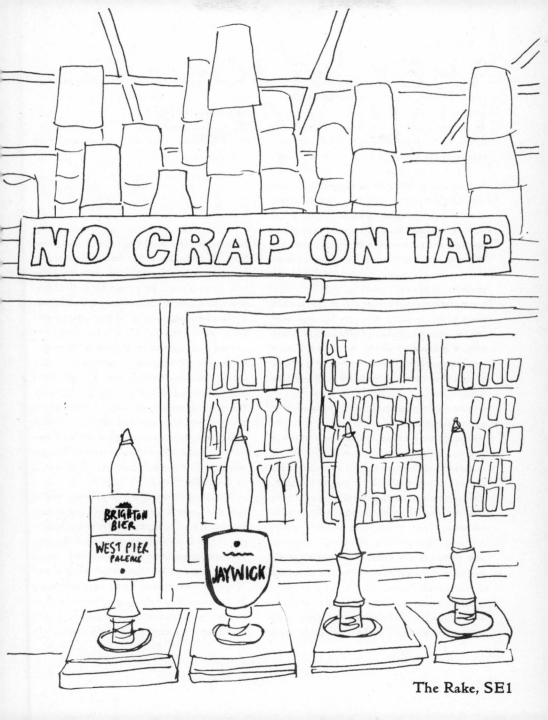

The Rake, SE1

visitor's bucket list. People travel far and wide to seek out their preconceived idea of a London pub. The old pubs of Dickensian lore, the location of the Leaky Cauldron or the one Bridget Jones lived above in the movies: you will of course find them here.

It sometimes seems hard to find a pub that hasn't offered extra-curricular adult services in the past, and they're still often used for dangerous liaisons. These were places for loose tongues, and often looser morals, with rooms rented by the hour for those in search of a cheeky knee-trembler. A sometime Elysian paradise for the working man of the day.

In more gentlemanly locales the world's maritime insurance industry sprang forth in the City of London's coffee houses and then the public houses. Soon the coffee was being offered with something a little stronger on the side, and the pubs became a fulcrum of burgeoning commercial activity. Business meetings, the peddling of wares and the beginning of mercantile exchanges – all found their home in the great pubs of London. Indeed, many a deal is struck and sealed across a tavern table to this day. City drinkers might be lucky enough to grab a seat at the bar, but the majority of imbibing is still done whilst vertical. Stand and deliver, we say! London is a bustling place of commerce, espionage and other acts – so don't get too comfy, as there is always another brilliant boozer just along the way.

Our pubs also provide a magical place to watch the famous Boat Race, drink where the laws of football were written,

or meet your future partner. The institution of the pub has survived temperance, two World Wars (and one World Cup). In the years following WWII the agent-general of Ontario, James S. P. Armstrong, was heard to comment:

'Bless the British licensed house. It saved our lives from loneliness – it is a glorious institution, and may it live and prosper forever.'

Whilst Paris might have its cafés, New York its delis, to understand London and the British people one has to push open the brass-handled door to the Great British institution known simply as the pub.

The character of each London neighbourhood helps to define the style of the venue. Pub-goers in Westminster might enjoy eavesdropping on politicos, those in Covent Garden rubbing shoulders with artisans and aspirant actors, those in Bloomsbury sharing bar room with academics and the intelligentsia. From a drink in the stately King's Head to the more down-at-heel Bricklayers Arms, there is indeed a pub for all comers.

Over the last ten years of professional pub touring (it really is a thing) we've been barred from a few, lost a handful of clients in the fog of war and even witnessed a marriage proposal. People from Tooting to Tonga have bonded over a few jars: a boozy United Nations trundling down Tippling Street with their kids and dogs and sometimes zero English in tow. God bless Google Translate.

After a few thousand pints we noticed

that people really, really like going to the pub, with the second most often asked question on our walks and wanderings being, 'What's your favourite pub?' So here are our musings. Our pantheon of pubs. This book is our love letter to London's liquid history, with a healthy serving of local legends and tall tales on the side.

Treat this book as an eccentric and eclectic pool to dip into, define your detour and hopefully find a handful to add to your very own little black book of boozing. From one-room ye olde wonders to the higgledy-piggledy and idiosyncratic, this book tries to cover them all.

Please note there is little mention of the exact drink offering, with no tasting notes attached. These attributes can change quickly, but we know you'll get a fair pint in each. Ardent wine lovers may need to look elsewhere, whilst beer aficionados will savour the resurgence in craft beer and microbreweries. London was once the biggest beer producer in the world, so when you sup a pint of porter in Borough Market or stand on the banks of the Thames and sink an IPA, the loop of history tastes that little bit fuller.

Fans of 'mother's ruin' will revel in the gin craze depicted in Hogarth's *Gin Lane*, and London's rise to becoming a world leader in the production of dry gin. Since 2009 changes in taxes and licensing (thanks to the dogged determination of the boutique distillers at Sipsmith) have seen a 'ginaissance' in small-batch production, with pubs returning to their gin-palace hey-day once again. Huzzah!

Gastronomic readers should by all means make a beeline for the Harwood Arms or the Eagle, but they veer a little too close to being restaurants to warrant inclusion here. The quality of food is so heavily determined by the incumbent chef that it can change at the drop of a hat. A pie at the Guinea Grill (p. 78) or a Sunday roast in many of the following establishments is a major draw, but only in addition to the main fluid fundamentals. Some of the pubs included do indeed have fine dining rooms upstairs or to the rear (just like Orwell's elusive Moon Under Water – see p. 192), but most survive with a wholesome selection of 'English tapas' including pork scratchings, Scotch eggs, pickled eggs, pies and sausage rolls – offering just enough substance to keep you vertical and resident at the bar a while longer.

This book presents a timeless selection for people who revel in the warmth of a real fire, a mug of good mild, genuine bonhomie and traditional innkeeping skills: those drawn by the pull of the handpump and those who insist cask is king. It is a book for those more interested in the background noise of clinking glasses and friendly chat, rather than piped muzak, giant TVs or flashing, beeping fruit machines. It celebrates places where dogs are guaranteed a warm reception, but children are entertained only at the landlord's discretion.

Whisper it, but you don't even need to be on the devil juice to enjoy a visit to the pub, and many of our clients leave as dry as the moment they arrived. This is a book also for people nonplussed by the vagaries *du jour*, for whom fashion holds little interest, but for whom the charm and enchantment of a cracking pub lasts eternal. Well-kept ale, wholesome food and friendly service form a simple but often overlooked holy trinity of earnest contentment. Each pub listed is placed in the context of its local area, highlighting a literary, architectural or other perspective, adding structure and definition to your otherwise wayward wanderings. History will be found on tap here as much as the beer, with each entry offering a fine example of its genre. These are perhaps pubs for those who prefer to look back in time more often than forward; a selection of pubs to be enjoyed by the culturally curious and those searching for an elusive chimera of authenticity. We'd honestly be delighted to have any of these pubs at the bottom of our street.

So it's an enormous 'Cheers!' for every client who has joined us for a trundle down Tippling Street over the last decade, shared an anecdotal nugget or perhaps indulged us with a pint or five. Come rain, snow or even some sunshine we've shared the most fantastic of times with groups ranging from solo travellers to over 100 people who appeared without notice in fancy dress!

A surprising number have even returned more than once to share a leisurely afternoon with our full gamut of *flâneurs* and storyteller guides. We start our walks as 14 or so strangers, often finishing as lifetime comrades. The record stands at 13 pubs and a gin distillery in a single stroll, so it's certainly been one hell of a knees-up.

Final thanks must go to the frontline London bar staff, surviving the long hours and low wages whilst continuing to offer the best of British hospitality with a healthy side serving of sardonic humour. We raise a glass to all those who share our love of this great British institution. We trust that you enjoy this book, for you were the inspiration for us writing it.

So sit back and enjoy our stumble in the staggering footsteps of Dickens, Shakespeare, Pepys and Johnson, whilst soaking up the sozzled history of the city at every tipsy turn.

And the best pub in London? It's each to one's own, with the perfect pub usually being the one just around the next corner.

And the most frequent question asked on our walks?

'Any jobs going, mate?'

LITERARY LEGENDS

'You find no man, at all intellectual, who is willing to leave London. No, Sir, when a man is tired of London, he is tired of life; for there is in London all that life can afford.'

Dr Samuel Johnson

*I*f writers didn't appear to spend so much time down the old rub-a-dub, just imagine the extra sonnets and short stories they might have conjured through the eons. Shakespeare dabbled in pub courtyards to perform for the penny-stinkers, whilst Dickens sought characterful inspiration sitting by many a London pub fire. Dylan Thomas even managed to lose a few manuscripts after one too many shandies. Writers and their subjects have flocked to pubs over the centuries, with every walk of life hosted, emotions roused and nefarious behaviour undertaken. Pubs make the perfect setting to write drama, meet fellow thirsty creatives and simply let the mind wander. Offering a microcosm of life, the whole world really is a stage, with the pub perfectly placed right at the very heart of it.

YE OLDE CHESHIRE CHEESE

ICONIC ALEHOUSE

'It was the best of times. It was the worst of times.'

Charles Dickens, *A Tale of Two Cities*

IF YOU CAN ONLY visit one London pub, make it this one. It is as much a part of London lore as red buses, black cabs, the chiming of Big Ben and Tube strikes. It truly puts the 'old' in 'ye olde'.

Seek out the illuminated lantern stating 'rebuilt in 1667' on Fleet Street to indicate an open door and a warm welcome. Then head down the arched corridor, passing the list of 15 or so monarchs that have reigned whilst this pub has been serving historically good times.

A truly mature cheese originally dating from the 1540s, this time capsule of consumption was rebuilt straight after the Great Fire in 1667. A gloomy higgledy-piggledy labyrinthine den of sawdust-strewn rooms fills this alehouse, often thick with the enveloping odour of the front-room fire. It is a place to escape the modern world, enjoy a little digital detox, and where quiet conversation still reigns. In *A Tale of Two Cities*, it is here that Charles Darnay celebrates his recently-won freedom with a 'simple supper and a few fine wines'.

Turn right as you first enter, noting the 'Gentlemen Only Served In This Bar' notice inscribed above the door, and imagine the inimitable Boz (aka Charles Dickens) sitting next to the fire – the portrait of the waiter of the time still hangs above the fireplace. Doff yer cap to 'Polly the Parrot' behind the bar and seek out the newspaper clippings regarding this African grey's notoriously sweary behaviour over 40 years, before she eventually popped her clogs in 1926 and took up a quieter, stuffed existence. If a simple pork pie and pickles can't sustain you in the beautiful murk of the front bar, then decant across the corridor to the Chop Room for simple fayre in equally atmospheric surroundings. The pub's world-famous pudding (think offal and oyster, not syrupy sponge) is no longer available, but an evening wrapped in the 'Cosy Corner' has an enduring charm.

This alleged one-time whorehouse (see the saucy tiles extracted from an upstairs room at the Museum of London) has seven bewildering warren-like storeys to explore, so venture down into the jumbled innards,

Ye Olde
Cheshire
Cheese
REBUILT 1667

Under 15 Sovereigns

Ye Olde
Cheshire Cheese
Rebuilt 1667
in the reign of Charles II
and continued successively
in the Reigns of

James II   1685-1688
Interregnum (until 1688-Feb)3 1689
William & Mary 1689-1702
                          1702-1714
Anne   1714-1727
George I   1727-1760
George II   1760-1820
George III   1820-1830
George IV   1830-1837
William IV   1837-1901
Victoria   1901-1910
Edward VII   1910-1936
George V   1936
Edward VIII   1936-1952
George VI   1952
Elizabeth II

GENTLEMEN ONLY SERVED IN THIS BAR.

enjoy a complimentary lobotomy on the low-hung ceilings, touch the charred beams, listen for the burbling Fleet river not far away, and imagine the many printers and journalists who have frequented these corners, to formulate tomorrow's headlines (whilst drinking on average six pints of strong beer a day). Until the 1920s tomorrow's news was sketched out over these humble tables, with the cavernous rooms providing a 'social network' for the Fourth Estate when the British Empire ruled one-fifth of the world's land mass.

Pictures of the great lexicographer Dr Samuel Johnson adorn the walls, and his chair rests in the Chop Room. Here, you can pay homage to Hodge, his oyster-munching feline friend, en route to Johnson's former home – now a museum – just around the corner. Known as a wig-wearing man about town, he was the author of weighty tomes, a hater of Scots, a possible Tourette's suf-ferer, icon of the *Blackadder* series, and the source of those timeless and sage old words . . . 'When a man is tired of London, he is tired of life.'

With no natural daylight penetrating the monasterial bowels of the pub, and an absence of clocks, the concept of time soon becomes an irrelevance. At over 450 years and counting, the Cheese is still proving quite the alcoholic mecca for pilgrims from both near and far. It is an incredible portal to the past.

Nowadays, the pub offers refuge for tourists, legal eagles and investment bankers seeking temporary asylum from the ever-modernising city outside. Note the well-worn front step as you rebirth yourself into reality, and remember not only Dickens, but also Conan Doyle, Twain, Thackeray, Johnson, Voltaire, Disney and more having entered before you. A true London legend and a true literary classic.

WHEN IN ROME: Get all wordy with the great lexicographer (and his cat Hodge) around the corner at **Dr Johnson's House**.

NEARBY & NOTEWORTHY: The Tipperary, The Old Bell Tavern, Punch Tavern.

 Chancery Lane & Blackfriars

 145 Fleet Street, Wine Office Court, EC4A 2BU

THE GEORGE INN

GALLERIED COACHING INN

'But first I make a protestation round
That I'm quite drunk, I know it by my sound
And therefore, if I slander or mis-say
Blame it on ale of Southwark so I pray.'

Geoffrey Chaucer, *The Miller's Tale*

THE ROMANS CLIP-CLOPPED their way past the front door of this pub and over the River Thames into Londinium around AD 43, followed by Chaucer's 14th-century pilgrims, before Shakespeare finally made it his local in the 16th century. The Bard often hired the courtyard prior to construction of his famous Globe Theatre along the riverside in 1599. Hundreds of people would squeeze into the yard and take their place amongst the penny-stinkers (the unwashed masses who paid a penny to join the crowd of pickpockets and charlatans) whilst the more affluent theatregoers would be afforded a less crowded view from the raised galleries.

The present-day building dates from 1676 and is the last remaining galleried coaching inn in the city. It is rightly Grade I listed – the same status as Westminster Abbey – and is owned by the National Trust. A slice of architecture so rare that only a third of the original building remains, leaving you to imagine the old inn encompassing all three sides of the yard. Horses would be stabled or reshod here, sustenance would be sought, and the galleried section of the inn would offer a room for the night – a precursor to the motel, if you like. Chaucer's *Canterbury Tales* begin at the long-lost Tabard Inn a few doors down; a successful pilgrimage to the tomb of St Thomas Becket is rewarded with a meal in that Southwark hostelry (see p. 186).

Dickens would also pop in en route to visiting his father in Marshalsea prison further down Borough High Street. Inspired by the characters observed here, the pub finds its own place in *Little Dorrit*, and Dickens' original life insurance certificate is framed next to the bar.

Even Sir Winston Churchill dropped in for a drink, but as a man of discernment he would not drink the local brew, instead bringing his own port and paying corkage.

As road journeys increased from 20 to over 100 miles per day with the advent of rail and motor vehicles, the use of inns was circumvented and as such all the infrastructure and stabling fell by the wayside. Thankfully, rather than being turned into a heritage museum, the George continues to do what it knows best and simply offers a welcoming pit stop to weary two-legged humans rather than the four-legged equine variety.

Don't forget to toast the boozing Bard on 23rd April, with St George's dragon-slaying antics handily tallying with the day of Shakespeare's believed date of birth and death.

Whether you want to relax in the idyllic sheltered courtyard during mild weather, or huddle by the creaky floor of the Parliament Bar on a winter's day, this is a venerable pub for all seasons.

WHEN IN ROME: Get all ghoulish at the **Old Operating Theatre**.

NEARBY & NOTEWORTHY: The Market Porter, The Rake, Royal Oak.

London Bridge & Borough

75–77 Borough High Street, Southwark, SE1 1NH

18

THE LAMB

SNOBBY

THE HANDSOME GLOSSY-GREEN tiled façade gives way to an atmospheric, immaculate, divided dark-wood interior. An oasis of London calm on bubbly Lamb's Conduit Street, where Admiral Nelson's chosen undertakers continue to trade, and medical staff from the nearby Great Ormond Street Hospital mingle at this much-cherished institution. The main pub partitions are largely gone but the famous etched-glass 'snob screens' survive, allowing customers to avoid eye contact with lowly staff, or for staff to avoid intimate contact with undesirables. A bit like going for confession, but with alcohol to lubricate the dialogue.

Dickens was a great commentator on class divides, and with his house around the corner is believed to have frequented the Lamb on a regular basis. What he made of the heavily divided pub, one can only imagine. Don't miss the small garden to the rear, the cosy snug, and the working polyphon (think Victorian jukebox) with the music-hall memorabilia remembering the pub in its A-list heyday. Note the pub's name, which comes from the Tudor man of status William Lambe, who built the conduit to supply the city with fresh water. His work was repaired by Sir Christopher Wren after the Great Fire.

A further literary connection arrives in the form of Ted Hughes and Sylvia Plath, who used the pub for early romantic assignations in the 1950s. Presumably the snob screens offered the requisite level of privacy for their romantic dalliances . . .

WHEN IN ROME: Toast the 'Inimitable Boz' at the **Charles Dickens Museum**.

NEARBY & NOTEWORTHY: The Queens Larder.

 Russell Square

 94 Lamb's Conduit Street, Bloomsbury, WC1N 3LZ

THE SPANIARDS INN

TOLLHOUSE TAVERN

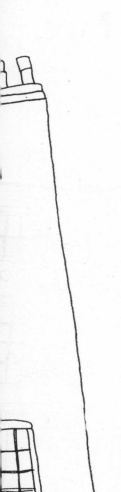

'What were Dick Turpin's famous last words?'
'"Whoa!"'

DATING BACK TO 1585 and featuring in both Dickens' *Pickwick Papers* and Bram Stoker's *Dracula*, this inn has layers of literary legend and ghost stories to unpeel at your leisure.

The building itself is famous for literally bringing traffic to a standstill, protruding into the road just as the nearby former tollgate does. And by the 18th century, where there were highways there was Dick Turpin. He is famously associated with this pub due to his father being a former landlord – and Dick himself was allegedly born within the four walls (keep taking those pinches of salt . . .). Give thanks that today the only hold-up is due to the cumbersome tollhouse narrowing the road outside and there is not a highwayman in sight. It's just the hooves of Black Bess, Turpin's horse, that can be heard riding late into the night as she haunts the pub's grounds . . .

To illustrate the purpose of inns in the day, it's worth noting that this location is a two-hour uphill drag from the City of London. The perfect pit stop for both man and beast. Even arriving on two feet from Hampstead Tube or from across the heath requires suitable restorative action to this day.

A capacious outdoor seating area, replete with a Fido-friendly wash, serves the dog walkers from the nearby heath well. But it's within the low-ceilinged, oak-panelled walls that one can imagine John Keats penning 'Ode to a Nightingale', Bram Stoker borrowing haunted tales to furnish his horror prose, or Joshua Reynolds enjoying the then unadulterated view as far as Windsor Castle on a clear day.

WHEN IN ROME: Drink to the Guinness family at **Kenwood House**.

NEARBY & NOTEWORTHY: **The Flask**, **The Holly Bush**.

⊖ Hampstead

🍺 Spaniards Road, Hampstead, NW3 7JJ

LAMB & FLAG

BUCKET OF BLOOD

Another Dickensian watering hole and former bare-knuckle boxing venue. The sign on the characterful alleyway reads thus:

'Stay traveller rest & refresh yourself in this ancient tavern within whose walls so many great figures of the past have taken their ease. Here often sat the immortal Charles Dickens and his friends, poor Samuel Butler & the wits and gallants of the restoration. Hither resorted the Bucks & Dandies to witness prize fights & rock mains, while hard by was enacted the notorious Rofe Alley Ambrusade in Derr 1679 when the poet Dryden was almost done to death at the instance of Louise De Kerouaille, Mistress of Charles II.'

WITH THE POET LAUREATE of the day beaten to within an inch of his life on the pub's doorstep, one might derive a lack of respect for the arts in the area. Ironically, the thesp-loving Garrick Club lies just across the street.

The mood does not noticeably improve inside either, with a cautionary Latin inscription running across the beams above the bar reading: 'My purpose is to die in a tavern, so that wine might be close to my dying mouth. Then a choir of angels will happily sing, May God be merciful toward this drinker.'

Nowadays, the ancient timbered building is wrapped in a later brick finish. This handsome façade gives way to a pleasantly dark interior with seating to the rear, and the upstairs hosts a fine selection of pugilist memorabilia. Most drinkers prefer to tumble down Rose Street on all but the most inclement of nights, enjoying the enclosed sanctuary set back from the main road. A truly historic pub standing strong in a sea of West End commercialism, mediocrity and terminal tourism.

WHEN IN ROME: Be star-struck at **The Actors' Church** of St Paul's.

NEARBY & NOTEWORTHY: **The Harp**, **The Nell Gwynne**.

 Covent Garden & Leicester Square

 33 Rose Street, Covent Garden, WC2E 9EB

25

THE FRENCH HOUSE

BOHEMIAN FRANCOPHILE

PHONES OFF! THE 'NO music, no machines, no television and no mobile phones' policy allows bohemian thinkers to converse and share wit amongst the black-and-white photo-bedecked backdrop.

If you fancy a leisurely pint then don't darken these doors. Only halves are served (except on their famous Pints Day, when you might spy Suggs from Madness behind the bar), and plenty of patrons prefer a glass of wine from our convivial continental comrades. Somewhat fittingly the upstairs dining room is often charged with Gallic gastronomy, and the kitchen is a famous breeding ground for some of the most influential chefs in London.

Run by the moustachioed Belgian Berlemonts from 1914 to 1989, it was formerly known as the York Minster, and during WWII became a refuge for members of the Free France movement. Charles de Gaulle popped by and possibly found inspiration for his rousing 'À tous les Français' work over a glass of rouge.

'The French' has been putting the boho in Soho for over 100 years, with its door open to whores, gays, publishers, flâneurs, actors, painters, pornographers, pimps and stagehands. It was an informal club for those who preferred its proletariat democracy over the nearby private clubs. Loyal patronage was repaid with informal cash advances offered from behind the bar as required.

With all this absinthe-fuelled bohemian excess, it is little wonder that Sylvia Plath signed and celebrated literary contracts here and Dylan Thomas left his only copy of *Under Milk Wood* after an all-day bender. Creative regulars included Francis Bacon and Lucian Freud, alongside the more surreal Salvador Dalí.

Visit on Bastille Day to revel in the full bon vivant flair. *Liberté, egalité, fraternité!*

WHEN IN ROME: Let them eat cake at **Maison Bertaux**.

NEARBY & NOTEWORTHY: **The Coach & Horses**, **Dog & Duck**, **The Lyric**.

 Leicester Square

 49 Dean Street, W1D 5BG

THE FITZROY TAVERN

1900s ENTREPÔT

'The Fitzroy is like the Clapham Junction of the world; everyone goes in and comes out at some time or other.'

Augustus John (painter)

THE FITZROY IS SO important that it shares its name with the area in which it sits, and from the 1920s to the 1940s it provided the cultural fulcrum around which bohemian London swung. It was 'the' pub du jour for the city's movers and shakers. The central fleshpot for the saucy Bloomsbury set who were said to 'live in squares and love in triangles'.

From its origins as a local coffee house to a later incarnation as the Hundred Marks (due to the local German population), it was given its present moniker after WWI.

People who went in and mostly came out included Dylan Thomas, Jacob Epstein, Michael Bentine, George Orwell and Nina Hamnett. This set of writers, composers and sculptors would pool the funds of their successes and drink until a lack of funds required further creative output.

Charity has always started at home here; iconic landlord Pop Kleinfeld set up the local charity 'Pennies from Heaven' in the 1920s, with customers attaching coin-filled envelopes to the ceiling of the pub via darts, and funds being distributed to needy local children.

The pub has been lavishly refurbished, now enjoying more room divides than perhaps practical or historically necessary. The bohemian kerfuffle may have decanted down the road to Soho in the 1950s, but you can soak up the old-school vibes in the Writers & Artists Bar, down a pint on the sunny street corner or review the literary heritage on the walls around you. The Fitzroy is well worth a visit. Or two.

WHEN IN ROME: Enjoy nostalgic play at **Pollock's Toy Museum**.

NEARBY & NOTEWORTHY: **The Wheatsheaf**, **Newman Arms**, **Champion**.

 Goodge Street

 16 Charlotte Street, Fitzrovia, WIT 2LY

THE COACH
& HORSES

NORMAN'S (JEFFREY BERNARD IS UNWELL)

A PLACE TO DRINK heavily and gossip even more. Two legends define the pub: Norman Balon (the landlord) and the journalist Jeffrey Bernard.

Norman started running the pub during WWII (1943) and lasted until 2006, often working 16-hour days for years at a time without a break. When asked what he would do on retirement he simply replied, 'Die.' Famous for being London's rudest landlord, he showed a steady stream of people the door for little to no obvious reason. His autobiography is simply titled *You're Barred, You Bastards*.

Jeffrey Bernard was an alcoholic low-life-loving journalist, recording the ins and outs of the pub and surrounding area in autobiographical form for his regular column in *The Spectator*. Jeffrey was said to have had a lot of wives, 'with at least four of them being his own'. Consuming 50 cigarettes a day and with a rapacious thirst for both horse racing and drink, he is probably best summed up, as always, in his own words:

> 'Without alcohol, I would have been a shop assistant, a business executive or a lone bachelor bank clerk. The side effects of my chosen anaesthetic have at least produced some wonderful dreams that turned out to be reality.'

Being Soho, every artist including Freud, Bacon, Hirst and Auerbach drank here. Peter Cook hosted *Private Eye* lunches here for nearly 40 years, and the publication's cartoons line the walls to this day.

The enduring spirits of debauched disdain may have left the building, but people still head here for comfort food, a jolly good knees-up and a rousing singalong around the piano.

WHEN IN ROME: Enjoy a strip at **The Cartoon Museum**.

NEARBY & NOTEWORTHY: **The French House**, **Star & Garter**, **Dog & Duck**.

 Leicester Square

 29 Greek Street, Soho, W1D 5DH

THE WHEATSHEAF

BOHO BOOZER

A TIPSY TRUNDLE FROM the Fitzroy Tavern with all its glitz and glamour lies the more bijou charms of the mock-Tudor Wheatsheaf. Appearing as a 500-year-old coaching inn but only dating to the 1930s, in terms of literary credentials it really is the real deal.

Legend suggests that George Orwell led the migration here from the Fitzroy Tavern, throwing up over the bar at least once whilst looking for a suitably low-life pub to make high-brow conversation in. Often escaping from his nearby work at the BBC to drink and discuss politics with the down-and-outs, the Newman Arms just up the road is said to have been the inspiration for the 'Proles' pub in his dystopian masterpiece *Nineteen Eighty-Four*. Orwell knew a thing or two about good pubs, and you can digest his yet-to-be-bettered magnus opus of musings on the subject to the rear of this book on p. 192. Pink china mug not included.

In 1936 a raffish Dylan Thomas stumbled into the pub and was introduced to a young Palladium chorus girl named Caitlin Macnamara. Thomas's tipsy head was soon resting in her lap declaring love and proposing wedlock. His whimsical words obviously worked wonders for they were in bed together a mere ten minutes later, and married within the year. The classic line of 'I'll have what he's having' has probably never been truer.

Propping up the bar with the 'Wheatsheaf Writers' was an array of artists and bohemians including Nina Hamnett, Julian MacLaren-Ross and Sting's very own 'Englishman in New York' Quentin Crisp. Read any of their biographies and you can fully immerse yourself in Fitzrovia's alcohol-fuddled heyday.

WHEN IN ROME: George Orwell fans might try to hunt out **Room 101** and visit his statue at Broadcasting House, whilst arty types shouldn't miss **Eduardo Paolozzi's mosaics** within Tottenham Court Road station.

NEARBY & NOTEWORTHY: The Fitzroy Tavern, **Newman Arms**, **Bradley's Spanish Bar** (Not a pub . . . but fun).

 Tottenham Court Road & Goodge Street

25 Rathbone Place, WIT IJB

2

THAMESIDE TAVERNS

'The Thames is liquid history.'

John Burns

Without the Thames, there would be no London. The river of kings is the basis for so much of the city's history and to walk its banks is a true joy. The historic navigation and entrepôt trading opportunities provided by the Thames make the riverside pubs amongst the oldest in the capital. Offering refuge to pirates and smugglers, providing viewing platforms for executions and acting as temporary studios for painters drawn to the ever-changing light, these establishments have in the past doubled as post offices, chandlers and prisons, but nowadays they're among the best pubs in London. Indeed there are few finer places to pontificate over a pint than these riverside boozers, which provide the perfect mellifluous surroundings to enjoy the ebb and flow of liquid history while paying homage to Old Father Thames.

THE DOVE(S)*

RULE BRITANNIA

IT'S HARD TO FIND a lovelier historical riverside watering hole; discovering the Dove is a bit like stumbling across Ye Olde Cheshire Cheese-on-Thames. Perched on a fine south-facing stretch of the river, it is history personified and a pub of superb antiquity. The establishment's early beginnings are not well recorded, but it is known that it made the transition from coffee house to licensed premises. Pedants will continue to suck the best legends from the history books, but the sense of time here is unmistakeable.

Charles II and his orange-selling mistress Nell Gwynne are unlikely to have ever visited, as local lore would suggest, because the pub was at that time yet to be built. However, had it been in existence it would no doubt have provided a fine riverside refuge for merry monarchs and their mistresses alike.

Upper Mall was an upmarket address in the day, and the houses you pass on the way to the pub (including that of the Arts and Crafts designer William Morris) are testament to the historic affluence of the area. As you stroll along the river, the narrow-paved approach provides an atmospheric entrance, with the sign above the door profiling prospective clientele with caution:

CHILDREN MAY NOT COME INSIDE
ALTHOUGH AN AWFUL LOT HAVE TRIED
COME INSIDE YOURSELF WE PLEAD
BUT KEEP YOUR DOG UPON A LEAD

* A riverside signwriter erroneously named the pub in the plural for a period of time, so it has been known as both singular and plural over the years.

Head through the often-missed door to the front bar, and you can enjoy what according to *The Guinness Book of Records* is the smallest bar in the UK. Three stools and a wooden bench fill a space 4 feet 2 inches by 7 feet 10 inches with ergonomic prowess. The snuggest of snugs. The brass plaque on the wall remembers the water level during the great flood of 1928 being disconcertingly high.

'As a result of old age and Hitler', the fireplace was rebuilt in 1948, and people who may have huddled around the hearth have included Ernest Hemingway, William Morris, Alec Guinness and possibly the poet James Thomson. Although it's not proven, the pub may have inspired Thomson to pen the words to 'Rule Britannia', and why should pure fact impede such an evocative tale? What we do know is that on leaving the Dove by boat he caught a chill, and died a few days later. A good excuse to linger at the fireside a while longer.

The much-coveted rear terrace offers a wonderful spot to be creative, amorous or cheer on the Boat Race crews as they swoosh past each year. Rule Britannia indeed!

WHEN IN ROME: Go to the source of London's liquid history and enjoy a tour of the **Fuller's Brewery**.

NEARBY & NOTEWORTHY: The Old Ship, Blue Anchor.

 Hammersmith

19 Upper Mall, Hammersmith, W6 9TA

THE PROSPECT OF WHITBY

THE DEVIL'S TAVERN

DATING TO 1520 AND staking claim to be the oldest riverside tavern, Turner and Whistler sketched views from the terrace of the Prospect of Whitby, and Dickens and Pepys were also frequenters. More regal drinkers such as Princess Margaret and Prince Rainier III of Monaco popped in to live like common people a little later in the pub's lifetime; whether they witnessed the cockfights and bare-knuckle bouts on the first floor no one can attest.

Steeped in legend and previously known as the Pelican and the Devil's Tavern (due to the ne'er-do-well patrons), it was rebuilt after a fire in the 19th century and renamed after the ship that used to bring coal from Newcastle and berth nearby. Only the original stone floor remains, but the ghosts of sailors, smugglers and pirates linger on: a noose hanging close to the riverside balcony window offers a reminder of the rough justice served here for over 400 years at Execution Dock. The infamous Judge Jeffreys was a local, and would have watched the final moments of those condemned to death from the pub. The victims drank a quart of ale prior to their demise as boats thronged the water, watching these famous gala events.

On a lighter, horticultural note, it is believed that the first fuchsia in the United Kingdom was sold in the pub for a tot of rum. After all, it's not all death and debauchery down on the old Wapping Wall.

Today you'll find a fine riverside terrace, panoramic upstairs rooms and a darkwood interior with a long pewter-topped bar. Ships' masts continue to prop up the building, 400-year-old stone flags line the floor whilst a human ulna bone found in the pub casually rests on a shelf.

WHEN IN ROME: Hunt for treasure with some **mudlarking** at low tide.

NEARBY & NOTEWORTHY: **Captain Kidd**, **Turner's Old Star**, **The Grapes**.

 Wapping

 57 Wapping Wall, St Katharine's & Wapping, E1W 3SH

THE GRAPES

GANDALF'S GAFF

'A tavern of dropsical appearance ... Long settled down into a state of hale infirmity. It had outlasted many a sprucer public house, indeed the whole house impended over the water but seemed to have got into the condition of a faint-hearted diver, who has paused so long on the brink that he will never go in at all.'

Charles Dickens, *Our Mutual Friend*

LOCATED IN WHAT WAS once the commercial centre of the British Empire, Sir Walter Raleigh is known to have embarked for the New World from just below the Grapes.

Dickens and Pepys also knew this 16th-century pub, with the former having a penchant for the table dancing that graced the snug on occasion. But it was also to this warren of wharves that Sir Arthur Conan Doyle sent Holmes to seek his opiate fix from the local Chinese immigrants.

The walls of the pub have a selection of local paintings, which is fitting; Narrow Street was once home to artists Francis Bacon (No. 80) and Edward Wolfe (No. 96), and Whistler dabbed his oils here too.

The most famous person in residence today is the inimitable Sir Ian McKellen. Co-owner and saviour of the pub, you might see the mighty Gandalf at the quiz night or stroking the stuffed cat given to him by his theatrical partner-in-crime Patrick Stewart. Enjoy the faux portrait of the owners on the wall, and be grateful that there are no fruit machines, piped music or other low-rent fluff. Gandalf's staff lies behind the bar, ready to keep any errant drinkers in line.

WHEN IN ROME: Don't miss Antony Gormley's sculpture *Another Time* on the foreshore.

NEARBY & NOTEWORTHY: The Prospect of Whitby.

 Limehouse

 76 Narrow Street, E14 8BP

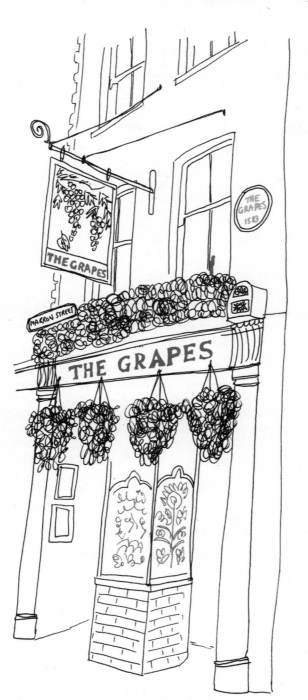

THE MAYFLOWER

PILGRIM POST OFFICE

THIS QUIET CORNER OF Rotherhithe is a portal to the New World: simply known as the Shippe from as far back as 1550, it was at this pub that the English separatists moored and prepared their boat the *Mayflower* on 6th September 1620, gathered together a crew and passenger list of around 100 people and set off, helped by a 'prosperous wind', on one of the most famous voyages in history. After a quick pit stop in Plymouth, by 11th November they had harboured in Cape Cod, and the foundations for the United States of America were laid.

The church of St Mary's opposite is where Christopher Jones, the ship's master, lies after returning in 1621. Several tablets, plaques and a windswept statue here remember his life. The church also hosts a communion table and chairs repurposed from the famous HMS *Temeraire*; a tangible sense of maritime history abounds.

After being rebuilt in the 18th century and renamed the Mayflower in 1957, the pub still remembers its forefathers. US stamps can be bought at the bar, remembering the time-starved sailors for whom a pint and a postage stamp was the order of the day.

Jonathan Swift's travelling Gulliver lived locally before setting off on his satirical adventures, and one likes to imagine him popping in for a tankard or two. Thoughtful mottos are inscribed on the walls and furniture, with olde worlde bric-a-brac completing the picture.

Relatives of the Pilgrim Fathers can prove their lineage and take their place in the book of Mayflower descendants, before retiring to the riverside terrace and sitting under the Stars and Stripes whilst getting their feet wet during the high-tide chop. Beware!

WHEN IN ROME: Marvel at 'the eighth wonder of the modern world', the Thames tunnel, at the **Brunel Museum**.

NEARBY & NOTEWORTHY: **The Angel**.

 Rotherhithe

 117 Rotherhithe Street, SE16 4NF

TRAFALGAR TAVERN

TAPPING THE ADMIRAL

Built on the former site of the Old George Tavern in 1837, no visit to Greenwich is complete without a flagon in this grand Regency palace that sits like an ocean liner atop the river wall.

Nelson himself didn't live to enjoy its riverside pleasures, having passed away at the Battle of Trafalgar in 1805. His body was pickled in a keg of naval booze to preserve him on the long journey home, but sailors made straws out of macaroni to drink from the barrel and by the time they reached Blighty, the barrel was dry. The drink was alleged to have a rather full-bodied flavour, and we can still enjoy a tot of Nelson's Blood, or navy rum, to this day.

On his return to dry land, Nelson's well-preserved body lay in state here in Greenwich. In the pub you will still find his portrait guarding the terrace, and his statue stands proudly outside.

Charles Dickens found the pub sufficiently grand to host the wedding breakfast in *Our Mutual Friend*, and the Liberal Party's famous whitebait dinners were also taken here. Politicians such as William Gladstone enjoyed eating the small fish straight from the Thames and they were served with iced champagne or punch until 1883. To many people the tavern still feels more like a grandiose spa town hotel than a drinking den.

With whitebait no longer found in the Thames and few liberals left in Parliament, this anchor of history holds its head high in the midst of the Maritime Greenwich World Heritage Site. Simply put, there is no better place to 'Tap the Admiral'.

WHEN IN ROME: Hunt down Nelson's musket-ball-ridden coat in the **National Maritime Museum** (see also **The Painted Hall**).

NEARBY & NOTEWORTHY: The Plume of Feathers, **The Cutty Sark**.

 Greenwich

 Park Row, Greenwich, SE10 9NW

CAPTAIN KIDD

PIRATE PUB

A YOUNG IMPOSTER AMONGST a number of historic Wapping taverns, this pub sprang into life from a converted coffee warehouse only in the 1980s.

In typical Samuel Smith's style, the landlords have conjured an evocation of time past; an innocuous opening on Wapping High Street leads through a courtyard and to a series of low-ceilinged rooms, flagstone floors and timber beams, making for an atmospheric place to drink. The relative youth of the pub is soon forgotten by the expansive joy of the riverside terrace.

This is a Thameside location where seafaring felons such as Captain Kidd were sent to their death until the mid-19th century. Having fallen foul of law changes regarding profiteering, Kidd met his maker here in 1701 following an unwise raid on an East India Company vessel. The stolen bounty was secreted off the coast of America prior to his execution back in England and is said to have inspired Robert Louis Stevenson's *Treasure Island*. The Admiralty publicised such executions widely, in order to deter others from committing similar misdemeanours. Guilty felons would be paraded through the streets, accompanied by a silver oar. Arriving at Execution Dock, the gallows were set below the low tide, indicating that they were under the jurisdiction of the Admiralty. After a swift ale to steady any nerves or smooth a confession, the ropes were set short, to encourage a prolonged death through suffocation. During Captain Kidd's execution the first rope snapped and he had to be rehung. Once dead, he was tarred to preserve his body, before being left in an iron cage suspended over the Thames for several years as a warning to ships' crews arriving and leaving London that might be tempted by piracy.

WHEN IN ROME: Visit the world's first police force, which dates to 1798, next door at the **Thames River Police headquarters** (by appointment only).

NEARBY & NOTEWORTHY: **The Prospect of Whitby**, **Turner's Old Star**, **Town of Ramsgate**.

 Wapping

 108 Wapping High Street, E1W 2NE

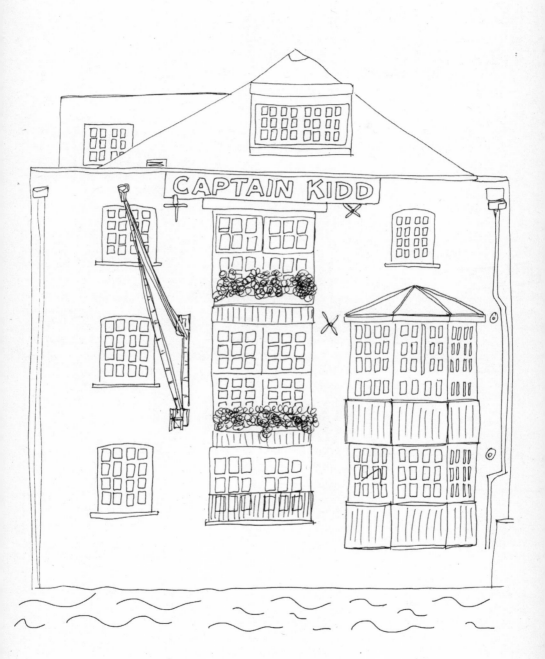

THE
ANGEL

THE ANGEL REBUILT C1337
IN ITS PRESENT FORM IS BY FAR
THE OLDEST TAVERN SIGN
IN ROTHERHITHE IT IS
RECORDED IN THE 8th CENTURY
AND MAY GO BACK TO THE MIDDLE
AGES THE ANGEL WAS ONCE SITED
DIAGONALLY OPPOSITE ALONGSIDE
THE MOAT OF KG EDWARD III's
MANSION BUT HAS LONG STOOD UP
THE RIVERFRONT NEXT TO
ROTHERHITHE OR KINGS STAIRS

THE ANGEL

10

BERMONDSEY WALL EAST

THE ANGEL

TURNER'S STUDIO

STANDING ALONE ON THE river wall, the Angel is one of Southwark's oldest pubs. Almost directly opposite the Captain Kidd (see p. 50), you could probably have watched the hangings at Execution Dock right here, and some people say that Judge Jeffreys, the infamous 'Hanging Judge' who dispatched up to 700 people for treason during the Bloody Assizes, did just that.

Built on the site of the 15th-century Bermondsey Priory, the place Pepys knew as 'the Famous Angel' is now a Victorian pub through and through. A divided dark-wood interior suitable for lovers of limbo dancing, leads to a small balcony right at the water's edge, with fine views back to central London and across to the Wapping Wall. The pub's panorama is wide, light and chock-full of atmosphere.

Captain Cook is said to have set sail for Botany Bay from here, and the pub could have provided a fine vantage point or possible inspiration for Turner to sketch *The Fighting Temeraire*. The skittish light dancing on the turbulent water can be truly magical here, and one can imagine the great artist sketching the Battle of Trafalgar warship being towed to the scrapyard in 1838.

Turner's painting marks the transition of time and power: a battle-weary champion being dragged to the knacker's yard, whilst the sun seemed to be slowly setting on the British Empire. Metaphors for life and mortality abound, but it was Turner's treasure. He called it his 'darling' and never sold it; rather, it was bequeathed to the nation upon his death. A special painting, and a special pub.

WHEN IN ROME: Don't miss the sculpture of *Dr Salter's Daydream* on the river wall adjoining the pub, highlighting the work of this healthcare pioneer and his tragic family tale.

NEARBY & NOTEWORTHY: The Mayflower.

 Bermondsey

 101 Bermondsey Wall East, Rotherhithe, SE16 4NB

TOWN OF RAMSGATE

THE LAST DROP

WAPPING WILL BE FOREVER linked with pilgrims, pirates and press gangs. The area's pubs, located in prime riverside positions at the top of the watermen's stairs, acted as job centres, chandlers and prisons for the passing trade.

Originally dating back to the 1400s, the Town of Ramsgate is famous as the place where the ruthless Judge Jeffreys was captured. After sending hundreds to their execution during the Bloody Assizes in 1685, the tide turned against his loyalty to James II and he was recognised as he tried to escape the country disguised as a sailor during the Glorious Revolution of 1688. A fitting finale would have seen him dragged down Wapping Old Stairs to Execution Dock, rather than to the Tower of London where he died by natural causes.

The link to Ramsgate is a result of happier times: fishermen from the Royal Harbour unloaded their catches here, rather than incurring the heftier landing taxes further up the river at Billingsgate Fish Market.

This pub has witnessed many exotic comings and goings, including Captain Bligh and HMS *Bounty*. Circumnavigating sailors were often greeted by the reassuring words still written on the pub wall:

> 'Your Polly has never been faithless
> she swears, since last year we parted
> on Wapping Old Stairs.'

WHEN IN ROME: Walk down to the foreshore during low tide, or enjoy the architectural splendour of **Wapping Pierhead**, built in the early 1800s for dock officials.

NEARBY & NOTEWORTHY: **Captain Kidd**, **The Prospect of Whitby**, **Turner's Old Star**.

 Wapping & Tower Hill

62 Wapping High Street, Wapping, E1W 2PN

3

BACKSTREET BOOZERS

'Sir, if you wish to have a just notion of the magnitude of this city, you must not be satisfied with seeing its great streets and squares, but must survey the innumerable little lanes and courts.'

James Boswell, *Life of Samuel Johnson*

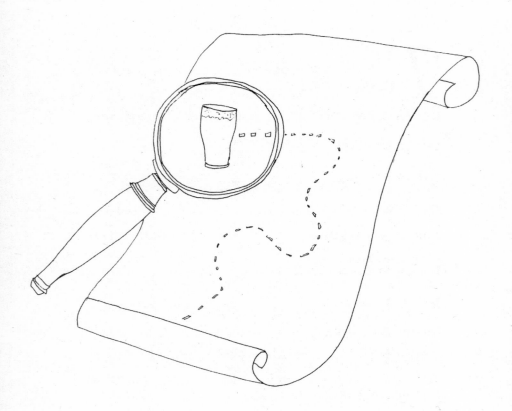

*T*he following are fine pubs where you expect them least. Proud to be amongst the hardest to find in the city, often hiding in plain sight from those that might live and work just around the corner. Perfect for surreptitious liaisons, hiding from undesirables or unwanted intrusion from bosses, these pubs' reputations are often held by those in the know. With lower natural footfall, you'll often find the hospitality that little bit warmer and more genuine. Dominant landlords, few tourists, good food and loyal clientele are the hallmarks of these gems. Rarely stumbled upon by chance, they will fill your 'little black book' and enhance your magical local knowledge no end, enabling you to impress friends and family with the words, 'I know this great little place just around the corner . . .'

YE OLDE MITRE

CAMBRIDGE GEM

NOT SO MUCH BACKSTREET boozer as seedy side-snook, and widely considered the hardest pub to locate in London (as well as one of the oldest, dating back to 1546), this historic alleyway pub is well worth the endeavour. Shoehorned between rows of diamond-sellers on Hatton Garden, head through the hole in the wall and leave the City of London for what was once considered the jurisdiction of Cambridge, formerly the grounds of the Bishop of Ely's palace. The pub was probably built for the servants of the bishop himself, and the estate would have run as an autonomous state akin to the Vatican. Ne'er-do-wells were known to escape into the alley, avoiding the clutches and jurisdiction of the City of London police. Perhaps fittingly, Fagin's den was located not far away, and the crime caper *Snatch* was filmed here too. Even the pub's licence had to be issued back in Cambridge until the 1970s.

The front bar contains remnants of the distinctive cherry tree used as a boundary marker and around which Elizabeth I is alleged to have danced the maypole with Sir Christopher Hatton. Locals often decant to the upstairs Bishop's Room or the rear snug, or imbibe *en plein air* huddled around giant beer barrels in the alley that handily doubles the size of the pub in fine weather.

Closed at the weekends, and offering a selection of English tapas in the form of Scotch eggs, toasties and sausage rolls, it is old-school enough for the ablutions to still be located outside.

Hidden in plain sight amongst London's famous diamond district, the most exquisite gem takes the form of a pub rather than a stone. Rare, exquisite and highly prized nonetheless.

WHEN IN ROME: Pop to **St Etheldreda's**, the oldest Catholic church in London.

NEARBY & NOTEWORTHY: **Bleeding Heart Tavern**, **The Jerusalem Tavern**, **The Viaduct Tavern**.

 Farringdon & Chancery Lane

 1 Ely Court, Ely Place, EC1N 6SJ

THE JERUSALEM TAVERN

ST PETER'S ALEHOUSE

DICKENS, JOHNSON AND PEPYS did not drink here: fact. (Although it has enough atmosphere to easily suggest they might have done.) We know this for sure as it was only repurposed as a pub in 1996. So it's the best con in London, and one we are more than happy to indulge in.

The building itself dates to the early 1700s and the wooden panels, tiles and platforms were added in the early 1990s to recreate the flavour of an 18th-century coffee house. It's more akin to a brown café in Amsterdam than a London pub. A splendid charade indeed, and a great example of how faux and pastiche can be achieved with true aplomb using the eye of an artisan. The epitome of good taste.

Another notable delight is that this pub provides the sole outlet for the estimable St Peter's Brewery in Suffolk, known for proffering its beer in characterful oval-shaped medicine bottles full of fruit-enhanced, cask-conditioned ales. This is an ale-lover's paradise, with the nectar often served from the wood.

The real bafflement comes from the fact that no one has tried or successfully managed to recreate this magic elsewhere in London.

The petite pub is divided into alcoves, booths and raised platforms allowing for quiet conversation, with the most coveted seats by the hearth. Due to its humble proportions, the crowd often spills out onto this otherwise quiet Clerkenwell street.

There have been at least three previous Jerusalem Taverns in this locality over the centuries, with patrons including Johnson, Hogarth and a young Handel. We're confident that if they'd been alive in Clerkenwell to this day, the new variant would provide more than ample hospitality.

WHEN IN ROME: Visit the **Museum of the Order of St John**.

NEARBY & NOTEWORTHY: **Ye Olde Mitre**, **Fox & Anchor**, **Bleeding Heart Tavern**.

 Farringdon

 55 Britton St, Clerkenwell, EC1M 5UQ

THE NELL GWYNNE

WEST END ALLEYCAT

NAMED AFTER THE INFAMOUS Drury Lane orange-seller cum mistress of Charles II, this is exactly the sort of murky local in which dangerous liaisons might have taken place. Both pub and mistress are equally tempting.

Handily placed off the thunderous Strand and the now chi-chi Maiden Lane, this is a wonderful backstreet boozer, perfectly located to wet your whistle with pre- or post-theatre drinky-poos.

The Old Bull Inn may have stood here originally, but now 'the Nell' continues good tavern ing for the modern drinker. Small, cosy, dark and friendly, this is a super sanctuary for the West End weary. Reminiscent of the Ship & Shovell (see p. 101) without its mirror image, you can even strike up the jukebox on the wall or gather around the piano.

Maybe 'pretty Nell' did know the former pub on this site, and the theatres are fittingly nearby, but there is little proof as ever. Modern doyennes such as Sienna Miller, as well as Jude Law and the ever-thirsty Richard Harris, have all been known to pop in for a pint of the black stuff.

But dark alleys hold dark secrets. On 16th December 1897, a disgruntled and unstable actor called Richard Archer Prince lurked in the shadowy doorway close to the Nell Gwynne. As the famous actor William Terriss approached the Adelphi stage door, Prince emerged from the shadows to violently stab him to death. The ghost of thespian Terriss continues to be spotted both at the Adelphi and at Covent Garden Tube station, the curtain never truly falling on his illustrious career.

WHEN IN ROME: Go for a meal or drink upstairs at **Rules**, the oldest restaurant in London. Old-school charm at its historic best.

NEARBY & NOTEWORTHY: **The Harp, Lamb & Flag, The Coal Hole**.

 Charing Cross

 1–2 Bull Inn Court, Covent Garden, WC2R 0NP

THE GRENADIER

HAUNTED MILITARY HIDEAWAY

LOCATED IN A PART of town full of oligarchs, embassy staff and residents from the swanky Lanesborough and Berkeley hotels, the joy of stumbling across this incongruous genteel treasure chest of booze on a quiet residential cobbled mews is a true revelation.

First-time visitors often feel they will be escorted politely from the Grosvenor Estate as they tiptoe their way behind the towering white icebergs of private real estate. The curious mind is rewarded with a cracker of a pub. Replete with sentry boxes outside, the upstairs floors were originally used as the officers' mess for the First Royal Regiment of Foot Guards, whilst the lower floors were hard-drinking and gambling dens for the common soldiers.

Both the Duke of Wellington and King George IV are said to have popped in, followed more recently by Prince William and Madonna, but the most famous presence at the bar is Cedric the ghost. This poor Grenadier was beaten to death for cheating in a card game and is said to haunt the pub to this day. The money-splattered ceiling is due to recent clientele leaving notes to pay off Cedric's gambling debts in an attempt to let him finally rest in peace.

It's not unusual to see modern soldiers toasting their fallen comrades, but you're as likely to come across private wealth managers using this discreet location to discuss liquid assets of another kind. Patriotically minded visitors from the UK will also enjoy the red, white and blue-themed paint job.

WHEN IN ROME: Visit No.1 London, aka **Apsley House**, the former family home of the Duke of Wellington.

NEARBY & NOTEWORTHY: **The Nags Head**, **The Star Tavern**.

 Hyde Park Corner

 18 Wilton Row, Belgrave Square, SW1X 7NR

THE NAGS HEAD

AUTONOMOUS MEWS FREEHOUSE

GIVEN THE ONLINE REVIEWS, this place should be sponsored by Marmite. People either love its homely informal charms or feel as if they've been personally hunted down and given the full Basil Fawlty treatment by the characterful landlord. It's his freehouse, his name above the door and he'll run it how he sees fit. It's his way or the highway in these boozy Belgravia backstreets.

The main tip is to refrain from using your mobile phone or any associated technology. Ignore this at your peril; the warm welcome could evaporate, and all manner of evasive actions may be required. Simply leave the building and take the call elsewhere (try Birmingham) if you can't forego communication with the outside world for the duration of a drink or two.

Probably best to hang your coat up, and don't take bulky backpacks or other bags.

One would surmise there is some general common sense and etiquette at play. Conversation and contemplation are enjoyed in equal measure, searching for a platonic ideal.

Strange as it may seem, it's worth treating this pub as a pub. It's not a tourist attraction, and don't try to bait the staff into action either. Go in, order a nice pint without too much faff, retreat to a lowly stool and engage staff and clientele at your leisure. Don't let the fact that the bar staff serve you from a sunken knee-high netherworld bother you. It's a lovely place: fires in the winter, bucolic bounteous baskets providing a flower-tumbling façade in the summer, vintage penny machines and bric-a-brac all year round; the interior is as uniquely characterful as the landlord and his locals in this village-like mews.

WHEN IN ROME: Deep-pocketed drinkers can quaff a cocktail in the **Blue Bar** at the Berkeley Hotel.

NEARBY & NOTEWORTHY: **The Grenadier**, **The Star Tavern**.

 Hyde Park Corner

 53 Kinnerton Street, Belgravia, SW1X 8ED

THE HAND & SHEARS

FIST & CLIPPERS

ON AN IDYLLIC 'lost in time' backstreet lies this beauty of a pub. In a handsome corner position, it is replete with an island bar and welcoming panelled and partitioned rooms. A quintessential corner boozer.

Legend suggests there has been a pub on this site since the 12th century, and the date above the door suggests it was established in 1532. Get creative after a few sherbets and you might imagine Charles II dining in the basement. Honest ales are served across the no-frills bar and simple ornamental decoration offers a quiet backdrop to the murmur of conversation. Sneak in the snug, hover by the fire, or spread out onto quiet Middle Street in the heart of the summer.

The name derives from the famous textile jamboree of Bartholomew Fair (1133–1855). The fair is said to have been opened by the Lord Mayor cutting the ribbon on the steps of the pub, leading to its moniker and to its nickname of the 'fist and clippers'. The pub was used during the fair for setting standard measures, issuing licences and settling disputes. The closing of the fair in Victorian times due to debauchery and public disorder brought much merriment to an end.

Men condemned to the gallows of nearby Newgate Prison would be brought here by wagon for their final drink. With only one drink (one for the road) allowed per man, their response to the offer of a second would be, 'No. I'm on the wagon.'

Even if that anecdote were proven to be a total untruth, this would be a charming, hospitable and welcoming stop for your last drink on earth. You really could do a lot worse.

WHEN IN ROME: Visit **St Bartholomew the Great**, the oldest church in London, and pass the former home of **Sir John Betjeman** en route.

NEARBY & NOTEWORTHY: **Rising Sun**, **Fox & Anchor**, **The Viaduct Tavern**, **Old Red Cow**.

 Barbican

 1 Middle Street, Smithfield, EC1A 7JA

THE SEVEN STARS

ROXY'S PLACE

A PLACE FOR LEGAL eagles to celebrate or commiserate with clients in the shadow of the Royal Courts of Justice. This is an idiosyncratic charmer of a pub, carved from a former wig shop and now bursting with bonhomie.

The 1603 date on the pub sign suggests Elizabethan heritage, and the vertiginous staircase does little to dissuade this idea. However, there's no ancient wooden-beamed interior to navigate; instead you'll find a bohemian brasserie full of checked tablecloths, theatreland prints, and the occasional cat appearing on the bar.

The name remembers the area being home to sailors from the Netherlands (formerly seven provinces), and the atmosphere is mostly dictated by the larger-than-life landlady, Roxy Beaujolais, formerly front of house at Ronnie Scott's,

West End doyenne, celebrity chef (note the cookbook behind the bar) and patron extraordinaire.

A small selection of ales is matched by well-curated wines by the glass. Shoehorn yourself in at the bar or escape to one of the adjoining rooms.

The complimentary bar snacks are best avoided as they are often cat food laid out to service one of the Elizabethan-ruffed feline friends named after late, great jazz artists and politicians including Ray Brown, Tom Paine and Clement Attlee.

Pause to enjoy eclectic signature dishes, or try one of the best dry Martinis in London: three shots of gin, vodka, vermouth, and a twist of lemon, pearl onion or olive. Roxy considers Martinis to be like women's breasts: one is too few; three too many. You have been warned.

WHEN IN ROME: Wander through the hallowed **Lincoln's Inn** and window-shop at London's oldest tailor, **Ede & Ravenscroft**.

NEARBY & NOTEWORTHY: **The George**, **Ye Olde Cheshire Cheese**, **Knights Templar** (for the ladies' bathrooms if nothing else).

 Temple

 53 Carey Street, Lincoln's Inn, WC2A 2JB

THE JAMAICA WINE HOUSE

THE JAMPOT

Man about town Samuel Pepys summed it up on his visit on 10th December 1660:

'... the first time that ever I was there, and I found much pleasure in it.'

JUST TO FIND THIS pub and explore the alley is joy enough in the heart of the ancient mercantile capital. A real zig-zag through labyrinthine turns is required to unearth this uniquely red sandstone-clad treasure.

The pub's location is known as the birthplace of London's coffee scene in 1652. Traders and businessmen flocked to this social network for conversation and commerce. With financial fingers in the West Indies, exploiting both sugar and slavery, this activity lends the place its Caribbean name. Away from the alcohol-infused alehouses, sober talk over coffee could lead to profitable trade, and for the price of a penny, the entrance and drinks were yours.

Stock and insurance brokers barred from formal exchanges due to their brash ways would converge on coffee shops to thrash out a deal. Notably, it is from Jonathan's Coffee-House nearby that the Lloyd's of London global insurance behemoth was founded.

Today, several centuries later, people gather at the Jampot to escape the offices and exchanges in the area – the pub still stands in the financial epicentre of both old and new London. Unfortunately, business practices have moved on, with a drink, handshake and the word of a gentleman no longer quite having the contractual gravitas it once carried.

WHEN IN ROME: Stroll through **Leadenhall Market** and savour the juxtaposition with the inside-out **Lloyd's** building towering above it.

NEARBY & NOTEWORTHY: **Lamb Tavern**, **Simpson's**, **George & Vulture**.

⊖   Bank

   St Michael's Alley, Cornhill, City of London, EC3V 9DS

THE RED LION

VILLAGE PUB

IF THE ROYALS LIVING in St James's or Clarence House need a swift half then this would be their local. Wonderfully shoe-horned amongst the private members' clubs of Pall Mall and the high-end retailers and auction houses of St James's lies this rufty-tufty unsullied little boozer. You could walk past the alleyway entrance for a lifetime and never know what unfettered joys await on this insalubrious cut-through. Legend suggests royal patronage has included everyone from Charles II (and the cellar named in honour of his mistress Nell Gwynne) to the Queen Mum, no doubt in search of her favoured G&T.

Secreted in a narrow arched alleyway, the Red Lion claims to be the last village pub in London and one of the oldest licensees in the area. It really is a fish out of water, but its modest charms drag everyone in, from local financiers to Monopoly pub-crawlers.

All are greeted with carpeted, wood-panelled charm and a small selection of beer. There's next to no food offering and the circuitous route to the ladies' loo on the upper floors implies that this has long been a traditional bastion of masculine backstreet boozing.

Visit on 30th January and you can drink surrounded by 'cavaliers' lamenting the death of their beloved monarch Charles I on this day in 1649.

Dogs are also usually welcome, so the local corgis could always join their regal owners for no-nonsense walkies and drinkies by royal appointment.

WHEN IN ROME: Pop to **Berry Bros. & Rudd** to sample the wares from London's oldest wine and spirits merchant, dating back to 1698.

NEARBY & NOTEWORTHY: **American Bar (The Stafford)**, **Duke's Hotel Bar** (birthplace of 007's Martini), **The Red Lion (Duke of York St)**.

   Green Park

   23 Crown Passage, St James's, SW1Y 6PP

THE GUINEA (GRILL)

MEATY MEWS

MOVE PAST THE MICHELIN stars, luxury boutiques and shiny showrooms of Mayfair and you will find this caught-in-time mews boozer churning out real ales and hefty meat dishes to those in the know.

Entering is akin to boarding a plane. Take the left-hand door and a top-hatted doorman will usher you past a fine display of steaks and into a time warp of prawn cocktails, world-beating pies and sticky puddings. The grill started in post-rationing 1952 to serve fine Scotch beef to the great and good (think Sinatra, Garbo, Minnelli) and to lingering Yanks left over from WWII. It remains so little changed that you could imagine Churchill and Eisenhower enjoying a claret-and-rump reunion in the corner.

Those light on time and in pocket can turn right into the pub bar. As Mayfair thrived in the 17th century, so did the demand to service the house staff from the grand town houses. Mews pubs were the perfect backstreet bolthole for the working class, nestled amongst the stables – hence the equine moniker.

The clientele may have gone up a social stratum or two, but a warm and welcoming boozer remains. Young's have been the landlord since 1888 and continue to dispense well-kept ales to the ever-spilling crowd. Those feeling peckish can still enjoy the pies and more at the bar without retiring to the rear for the legendary mixed grill or Sunday lunch.

A vegan's nemesis awaits.

WHEN IN ROME: Visit the **Handel & Hendrix** museum to see how one wall and 200 years separated these noisy neighbours.

NEARBY & NOTEWORTHY: **The Windmill**, **The Coach & Horses**, **Iron Duke**, **The Connaught Bar**.

 Green Park

 30 Bruton Place, Mayfair, W1J 6NL

THE SHIP TAVERN

PRIEST HOLE

A PUB THAT LOOKS to have turned its back on busy London. Exiting Holborn Tube station, or ploughing down Kingsway, people have little idea that this corner gem awaits the parched perambulator.

The location on Gate Street remembers the nearby Lincoln's Inn Fields being used for cattle grazing until the 17th century, with turnstiles allowing pedestrian access. Thirsty field workers would have known the original inn well. These narrow rat-runs are in fact the secret of the pub's success, allowing access only on foot for the discerning drinker.

The current building dates to 1923, but the pub's history remembers 1549 – a time when persecuted Catholics would

seek refuge here, with priests dispensing Mass from behind the bar. If the King's men were spotted, the priest would withdraw to his hidey-hole in the cellar whilst the congregation could pretend to be enjoying a jolly good drink. Unlucky priests who were caught and summarily executed on the spot are said to make the occasional apparition to this day.

Nowadays, a bustling mix of drinkers worship here seven days a week, alongside the occasional Freemason, with a lodge consecrated here in 1786. Upstairs hosts a fine candlelit dining room, and Sunday brings the famous gin-and-jazz sessions with over 50 different juniper-infused tipples behind the bar.

WHEN IN ROME: A visit to the exquisite **Sir John Soane's Museum** is unmissable: art, architecture and a healthy dose of eccentricity.

NEARBY & NOTEWORTHY: Princess Louise, Holborn Whippet, Cittie of Yorke.

 Holborn

 12 Gate Street, Holborn, WC2A 3HP

THE HOLLY BUSH

HAMPSTEAD HIDEAWAY

BEING EASIER TO FIND on foot than by car is usually a good sign. The steep journey via path or stairs to the Holly Bush allows you to take in the refined and affluent air of the liberal Hampstead elite. It's generally all uphill, but your thirst is easily sated on arrival by this cracking hostelry full of nooks, snugs and firesides.

Perfectly poised in the imagined London of Hollywood film-makers, with narrow cobbled streets, lanterns and period architecture all around, even the pub's interior was gaslit until recently. Surrounded by some of the wealthiest residents in town, the Holly Bush offers a relaxed and almost rural charm to the area, with dogs being as welcome as humans after their walkies on the nearby heath.

The bohemian local crowd means the pub has witnessed numerous luminaries, including Michael Faraday hosting gaslit debates on the merit of electricity and John Constable hosting art lectures. Even Dr Johnson and James Boswell are said to have paused for an ale or three.

The pub was formerly a stable block, then catering arm for Romney's House next door before striking out solo as a tavern in its own right. Once described as 'a dirty heaving centre of drunkenness', other than the occasional ageing rock star misbehaving this is a wonderfully civilised backwater in which to enjoy a pie and a pint. Just beware the resident ghost posing as a waitress who always takes your orders yet never delivers.

WHEN IN ROME: Pop to **Fenton House** for 17th-century merchant grandeur, or for more contemporary matters head to **2 Willow Road** for Ernő Goldfinger's controversial modernist masterpiece.

NEARBY & NOTEWORTHY: The Flask, The Spaniards Inn.

 Hampstead

 22 Holly Mount, Hampstead, NW3 6SG

THE QUEENS LARDER

BY ROYAL APPOINTMENT

THEY SAY THE WAY to a man's heart is through his stomach, and this pub bears testament to that. George III received treatment for his infamous sporadic bouts of 'madness' at the nearby premises of his medical practitioner Dr Willis. Doting Queen Charlotte would aid his care by nursing and cooking for him. She hired the pub's cool cellar space to keep his favoured foods in and to act as a temporary royal larder. The experimental treatment of her husband often included cold baths, beatings and starvation, making her loving gesture all the more heart-warming.

The Bloomsbury area is known for its universities and medical services to this day, with many clientele emanating from these fields. Great Ormond Street Hospital lies across the way, and the statue of Peter Pan at the hospital entrance acts as a reminder of J. M. Barrie's remarkable donation of all royalties from 'the boy who never grew up' to the children's hospital.

The pub itself is small and homely, having been carved from a large domestic property. The pedestrian alley alongside is an antiquated joy, and the square itself is one of London's finest idylls. Named after Queen Anne rather than the Queen Charlotte linked to the pub, the gardens offer a peaceful respite for those either suffering or serving those that suffer. Robert Louis Stevenson once remarked of the local area, but it could easily apply to the pub itself, that it seemed to have been set aside for the 'humanities of life and the alleviation of all hard destinies'.

WHEN IN ROME: Explore the **Foundling Museum's** role as the UK's first children's charity and public art gallery.

NEARBY & NOTEWORTHY: **The Lamb**, **Princess Louise**, **The Ship Tavern**.

 Russell Square & Holborn

 1 Queen Square, Bloomsbury, WC1N 3AR

ARCHITECTURAL ICONS

*'I don't know what London's
coming to – the higher the buildings
the lower the morals.'*

Noël Coward

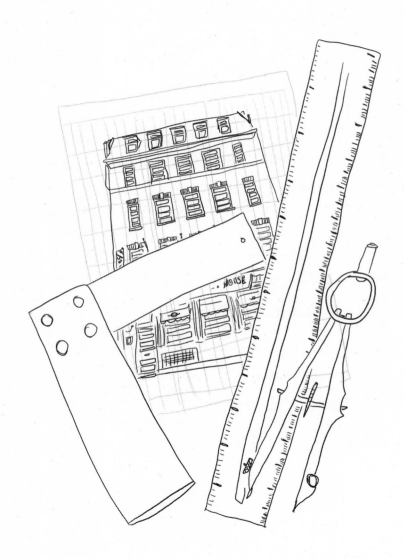

*C*hosen for the unique architectural flair they bring to the capital, these reminders of times gone by bear testament to when breweries were financial powerhouses keen to show off their wares and market them accordingly. From art nouveau gems to baronial banqueting halls, many were built when Britannia really did rule the waves and the city had a taste for the opulent. Thankfully now listed heritage buildings in the main, they have survived not only the Blitz but also post-war demolition to offer edifices of sculptural and decorative magnificence. A couple of choices still have reminders of the British class system still in evidence. Enjoy them all: they will never be built again.

THE BLACK FRIAR

ARTS AND CRAFTS GEM

'It's strange that those we miss the most,
are those we take for granted.'

Sir John Betjeman

APPEARING AS LONDON'S STAND-ALONE equivalent to New York's famous wedge-shaped Flatiron Building, our version dates to 1875, with the interior crafted by one of the top artists of the day in 1905 – Henry Poole of the Royal Academy. The budget would appear to have been almost limitless as he unleashed over 50 types of marble, stained glass, mother-of-pearl and metal reliefs with wild abandon. His only pre-condition was to remember the lives of the Dominican monks who inhabited this verdant section of the riverside from the 13th century onwards, making the establishment one of the world's first ever theme pubs. A shimmering example of Edwardian fantasia.

Behind the bar the inscription reads, 'Tomorrow Shall be Friday' – a day of fasting in the Catholic church and abstinence from meat, hence the accompanying depiction of monks going fishing. Further reliefs show carol singing and harvesting,

and the more you look the more exquisite details reveal themselves. Head through the three marble archways and enjoy the secluded Byzantine-style dining chamber. Irreverent witticisms proclaim 'Haste Is Slow, Finery Is Foolery, Don't Advertise, Just Tell A Gossip', whilst yoke-wielding monks gaze down on you from on high in between the light fixtures. Hunt out the incongruous Humpty Dumpty and bear-and-the-honeypot carvings, and don't miss the Lilliputian scene in the alcove with sleeping giants and lantern-carrying nymphs. Truly exquisite.

Nouveau butterfly motifs, marble clocks and window frames complete the picture of lavish indulgence, and the layers of nicotine accumulated over 100+ years (check the ceiling hue) have not tarnished the establishment's grandeur.

Note the difference between the public and saloon bars, with a reminder in the form of a raised single slat of wood above the former's doorway. There's marble and bronze in the saloon, and a more under-stated wood décor for the public area. The exterior monks give class-profiling directional guidance on entry, and the outdoor mosaics are worth admiration in their own right.

No wonder the rotund monk at the prow of the building looks so jovial: he knows the ostentation and hospitality that lie inside – traits noted by the papal magistrate visiting Tudor London to discuss Henry VIII's divorce from Catherine of Aragon, and possibly why he chose to stay at the Blackfriars monastery, the purveyors of the best food and drink in the city.

Before you leave, raise a glass to the Poet Laureate Sir John Betjeman, who helped save this pub (and St Pancras station, amongst other fine buildings) from demolition in the 1960s. A conservationist visionary of the day, he rescued this beauty from extinction. If you've ever wondered what use poets are in modern society, now you have your answer: they save our pubs.

WHEN IN ROME: Settle into the pub's **'Saturday Afternoon'** dining room for historic fish and chips in one of London's finest venues. A special and slightly bonkers place indeed.

NEARBY & NOTEWORTHY: The Cockpit, The Old Bell Tavern, Ye Olde Cheshire Cheese.

 Blackfriars

 174 Queen Victoria Street, EC4V 4EG

FOX & ANCHOR

A NIGHT ON THE TILES

STAND ACROSS THE STREET and admire this handsome and remarkable four-storey Smithfield treasure. The façade is resplendent in elaborate tiles from the Royal Doulton ceramic company of Lambeth, and grotesques punctuate the astonishing pastel exterior. Shopping or foodie aficionados might recognise this signature work (by William J. Neatby) from the Harrods food hall; so you know you shall be drinking in fine style.

Enter the 1899 Arts and Crafts treasure, where a narrow bar awaits. It's often best to take your pint *en plein air*, or grab a hearty bar snack and settle into the tiny snugs to the rear of the pub, now known as the Fox's Den. The whimsical pub name, emanating from a fox making stowaway via a ship's anchor, adds to the quixotic charm.

The walls are hung with vintage photos from the last remaining historic wholesale meat market of nearby Smithfield, and this pub is one of a handful famous for opening early in the morning to service the thirsty market porters finishing their shift. The current owners still open at 7 a.m. for anyone in need of a hearty breakfast and possibly a tankard of ale (technically for market workers only, but open to loose interpretation). A breakfast of champions inside Arts and Crafts grandeur par extraordinaire.

WHEN IN ROME: Visit the bubonic plague pit of **Charterhouse Square**, home to over 50,000 victims, and the monastery itself which dates to 1348.

NEARBY & NOTEWORTHY: **The Hand & Shears**, **Old Red Cow**, **Rising Sun**, **The Jerusalem Tavern**.

Barbican & Farringdon

  115 Charterhouse Street, Clerkenwell, EC1M 6AA

PRINCESS LOUISE

GLAM GIN PALACE

HIDING IN PLAIN SIGHT on this thumping thoroughfare lies the finest gin-palace-style pub still in existence. Built in 1872 and named after the rebellious fourth daughter of Queen Victoria, the architecture remembers a time when the British Empire covered around two-thirds of the earth's land surface. Even the glacial blue majesty of Canada's Lake Louise was named in the princess's honour. Try to imagine an alcohol-themed Royal Albert Hall or V&A Museum and you should get the idea. Not to everyone's taste, but there can be no denying the level of gaudy detail and ambition here.

No surface is left unadorned: there's a rhapsody of mosaic floors, etched glass, etched mirrors, Victorian tiling galore, wrought ironwork and a masterpiece of a ceiling. Gentlemen are even afforded the simple pleasure of urinating on a Grade II listed building when they visit the famous bathrooms. Constructed from solid marble, with a natty tiled floor, it authentically whiffs of the 19th century down there too.

Lying close to the parish of St Giles, one of the worst 18th-century slums in London, as depicted in Hogarth's *Gin Lane*, for the price of a pint the common man or woman could enter to enjoy a regal finery that was otherwise only imagined. Even the electric lighting would have been a source of marvel and delight in comparison to their dank, soot-ridden homes. Now it offers a touch of West End disco-ball razzle-dazzle and gin-palace bling.

The extensive use of elaborate partitioning divides the pub into a puzzle of snugs, public bars and privacy bars. There is a room upstairs with little architectural feature of note, but it did allegedly play host to the Rolling Stones and Bob Dylan in the day. This might explain the cracks in the beautiful *fin de siècle* ceiling.

WHEN IN ROME: Take a stroll down **Denmark Street (Tin Pan Alley)** and remember Bowie, the Stones and Elton in their bohemian heyday.

NEARBY & NOTEWORTHY: Holborn Whippet, The Ship Tavern, The Cross Keys.

Holborn

208 High Holborn, WC1V 7EP

THE SHIP & SHOVELL

A PUB OF TWO HALVES

No, YOU'RE NOT SEEING double. This is the only pub in London divided into two individual parts, on opposing sides of the street but with a shared cellar. A pedestrianised pathway splits the two, providing a delightful thoroughfare in which to sup a fair-weather pint. Nautical themes abound: head for the Crow's Nest function room to remember Sir Cloudesley Shovell rising from cabin boy to admiral before embarrassingly scuttling a Royal Navy fleet on the rocks off the Isles of Scilly. Beer ahoy!

There is no suggestion that J. K. Rowling sought inspiration here, but think of it as a Diagon Alley of drink. Squeezed characterfully between some charming period houses, there may be no butter-beer available but the place does manage to exude a magic conviviality all of its very own.

It's a very British thing to celebrate heroic but epic failure, and this pub sums it up. Sir Cloudesley was responsible for the most impressive naval calamity this fine maritime nation has ever seen. Yet he is remembered fondly and he has this fine pub named after him. There are many things to toast here, including a celebration of Christmas during summer so that the workaday rat-race patrons can enjoy their own festivities; but you can't beat raising a glass to a truly infamous foul-up. Here's to glory, honour and heroic failure!

WHEN IN ROME: Pop to **Benjamin Franklin's former house** around the corner. Often attributed with the memorable quote, 'In wine there is wisdom, in beer there is freedom, in water there is bacteria.' We'll drink to that.

NEARBY & NOTEWORTHY: **The Harp**, **Gordon's Wine Bar**.

 Embankment

 1–3 Craven Passage, WC2N 5PH

THE CHURCHILL ARMS

FLOWERY

> '**Most people hate the taste of beer – to begin with.
> It is, however, a prejudice that many people have
> been able to overcome.**'

Winston Churchill

IT REALLY IS HARD to see the pub for the trees here. Come Christmas time it's festooned in nearly 100 trees and over 20,000 lights. So bright you can see it from space! (Okay, we made that up – but you get the idea.)

Summertime drinkers will be equally impressed by the floriferous bounty, with the façade bedecked in a tumbling kaleidoscope of blooms. Hay fever sufferers approach with caution!

A cornucopia of memorabilia will delight Churchill fans. The link to the great man himself is of course tenuous, with his grandparents being regulars here and the pub only renamed in his honour after WWII. The downing of pints of Pol Roger champagne from silver tankards in the style of Winston himself is a forgotten excess. The fizz-pop was often his crutch; as he quipped, 'In success you deserve it and in defeat, you need it.'

Legendary landlord for over 30 years, Gerry O'Brien, may have pulled his last pint of London Pride, but the alchemy of the 'hanging gardens of Kensington', mixed with local vibes and the slightly incongruous but deliciously authentic Thai menu, lives on. The ultimate fusion of British history, mixed with strong Irish character, and finished off with the flavours of Bangkok. An experiment in mixology that's unlikely to be replicated with success elsewhere, but that's all part of the eccentric charm.

A homemade historic blue plaque records the mad spirit of the place. Tongue-in-cheek, but fitting all the same:

> '**Churchill made his wartime
> broadcasts here, and laughed at
> Hitler's watercolours while drinking
> banana daiquiris and farting.**'

WHEN IN ROME: Work up a thirst in Holland Park or Kensington Gardens. Culture vultures might head to **Leighton House** and the **Design Museum**.

NEARBY & NOTEWORTHY: The Windsor Castle.

 Notting Hill

 119 Kensington Church Street, Kensington, W8 7LN

CITTIE OF YORKE

CAVERNOUS

THE BUSY ROAD OF High Holborn and a handsome Portland stone façade offer little inkling of the barn-like interior that awaits. Tudor, Victorian and Edwardian touches can all be seen here, with the early 20th-century overhaul eschewing the vogue for Victorian gin palaces in favour of dark and grand neo-Tudor excess. Perhaps a war-weary Britain yearning for comforting solidity and nostalgic architecture.

The pub was built on land owned by Henry VI and dates to at least the 1400s. The narrow hallway leads to a cavernous medieval-style great hall, reminiscent of a Tudor banqueting hall; you might expect Shakespeare's players to emerge and rattle through *Twelfth Night* at any moment. Formerly known by Dylan Thomas (no stranger to alcohol) as Henneky's Long Bar, even Dickens' David Copperfield had lodgings next door.

Voluminous casks, holding between 500 and 1,100 gallons, levitate above the bar whilst railway carriage-style seating allows areas of almost confessional-like atmosphere for lawyer and client to enjoy a private tête-à-tête. Oddities continue with the freestanding cast-iron ornamental

fireplace at the centre of the room. With no sign of a chimney (hidden within the floor) or fathomable rhyme or reason for its random location, it remains a delightful enigma to this day.

Agoraphobic drinkers can descend to the more intimate confines of the cellar bar. It is said that people fleeing the Gordon Riots during the 18th century sought refuge here. The unusual acoustics from the curving roof allow for excellent eavesdropping opportunities... Looser-tongued drinkers might want to heed the inscription, 'In Vino Veritas' – in wine there is truth.

WHEN IN ROME: Admire the Tudor architectural finery of **Staple Inn** dating back to 1585 just across the road.

NEARBY & NOTEWORTHY: Ye Olde Mitre, The Ship Tavern, The Queens Larder.

⊖ Chancery Lane

🍺 22 High Holborn, WC1V 6BN

THE PRINCE ALFRED

MACHIAVELLIAN

A CRACKING PUB IN the midst of grandiose mansions exuding understated opulence. It's as if the Princess Louise (p. 96) has been shrunk and faded a little in the tumble dryer, losing some of the lavish embellishment. Perhaps consider it the ugly brother, but still very charming all the same.

Appearing as an epic architectural undercut, the jagged and curving con-certina glass frontage is beguiling and seemingly supports three storeys of prime West London estate. It gives way to an eccentric and somewhat confusing se-lection of mahogany-divided rooms. Limbo experts can duck and bob between the sec-tions, whilst shy types will enjoy the rarity of the all-but-forgotten snob screens. Lavish etched glass, tiling, mosaics and timepieces abound, offering Victorian craftsmanship at its best. There is a strong whiff of ecclesiastical excess, classically informed touches and hints of academia about the carved partitions. Perhaps even a whiff of courthouse grandeur too?

On a tangent, David Bowie fans might get a sense of déjà vu, with his short film *Jazzin' for Blue Jean* and the music video for his song 'Blue Jean' featuring the pub.

The rear dining rooms offer modern reinvention for the masses and a speakeasy-style dining space in the old coal cellar completes the picture for one of the most intriguing architectural pubs in London.

WHEN IN ROME: Take a waterside wander around **Little Venice** and on to Camden, or seek out the blue plaque for 'king of the code breakers' **Alan Turing**, born just around the corner.

NEARBY & NOTEWORTHY: **The Warrington**, **The Warwick Castle**.

Warwick Avenue

 5A Formosa Street, Little Venice, W9 1EE

YE OLDE WATLING

CITY SURVIVALIST

DESTROYED BY THE GREAT FIRE in 1666. Rebuilt in 1668. Damaged during WWII. Restored in 1947.

This is a pub with real staying power, built upon, and named after, one of the most famous Roman thoroughfares, dating back to AD 47. The famous Watling Street ran all the way from Dover. It spliced through the heart of Londinium, on to St Albans and eventually culminated close to the Welsh border a few hundred miles away. The only nod to the pub's Roman heritage is a resplendent centurion's helmet adorning the hanging pub sign and the narrow street dimensions imitating the ancient road layout to this day.

Commanding a wonderful corner site in the historic leatherworking quarter, modern day drinkers ebb and flow across the quiet cobbled streets. Step inside and the chunkily dimensioned dark beams are said to be repurposed from brine-pickled ships' timbers, procured not far away from the banks of the River Thames.

More famously the great architect Sir Christopher Wren is noted for using the upstairs rooms here whilst constructing St Paul's Cathedral for over 35 years. A place to roll out his plans, commune with his masons and more importantly provide them with food, shelter and liquid refreshment downstairs. Building cathedrals can be hungry work, and stonemasons like Roman armies obviously march on their stomachs.

As you leave, step outside onto Watling Street and gaze uphill to enjoy a magnificent view of the cathedral. It soon becomes apparent that to build a fine cathedral, you must first build a fine pub. Amen.

WHEN IN ROME: Travel back over 1,800 years to visit the **Temple of Mithras** and view over 600 Roman artefacts pulled from the subterranean Walbrook river.

NEARBY & NOTEWORTHY: **The Jamaica Wine House**, **George & Vulture**, **The Cockpit**.

Mansion House

 29 Watling Street, EC4M 9BR

YE OLDE COCK TAVERN

NARROW

WITH A MONIKER THAT makes it a particular favourite for hen parties, this building viewed from afar really is a charming sight. Appearing like an architectural skyrocket squeezed into its silo ready for lift-off, the timbered building claims to be the City of London's narrowest pub.

It feels like we've been teletransported into continental Europe, where they seem to have become past masters at shoehorning such buildings into their grand squares. The pub itself crams an enterprising amount of bar room and seating into the several floors.

As a full disclaimer, the true joy of this pub is on the outside rather than within. Those of keen eye might seek out a historic wooden mantelpiece, said to be several hundred years old; but the tavern's current incarnation only dates to the late 19th century, with the real history being in its former glory at its original site across the street.

The original Cock & Bottle, as it was known, was frequented by Tennyson, Dickens, and of course Fleet Street stalwart Dr Johnson. Samuel Pepys diarised his salacious assignations with female conquests here, so it was obviously quite the social fulcrum. However, it was flattened for the arrival of the Old Bank of England in 1886 and moved across the street. Many original fixtures and fittings were reinstalled, including carvings possibly by the one and only Grinling Gibbons. Unfortunately a fire in 1990 destroyed the majority of these pieces, but you can simply enjoy the pub's towering slimline nature and toast its legend and ongoing survival.

WHEN IN ROME: On weekdays *Da Vinci Code* conspirators should take a walk to **Temple Church**, and pass **Middle Temple Hall** where Shakespeare premiered *Twelfth Night*.

NEARBY & NOTEWORTHY: The George, **Ye Olde Cheshire Cheese**, **The Tipperary**.

Temple

 22 Fleet Street, EC4Y 1AA

YE OLDE COCK TAVERN

THE OLD BELL TAVERN

WREN'S MINI-MASTERPIECE

SIR CHRISTOPHER WREN IS one of the most venerated British architects of all time, famed for building the iconic St Paul's Cathedral and other edifices including the Royal Hospital and a remodelling of Hampton Court. His architectural talents are well known, but his business acumen less so. When building a church, he would often build a pub next door. Jackpot!

During the day he would pay his stonemasons to chip away at his next church, but at night he would offer them a place of warmth, shelter and plentiful drink. Of course he'd be receiving a good proportion of wages back across the bar. The church of St Bride's was known as one of the fastest to be completed after the Great Fire in 1666 due to the proximate hospitality provided by the neighbouring tavern. The pub itself is small in stature, but immensely charming. A central curving bar dominates the dark-wood rooms, full of subtle level changes and fireside snugs. A beautiful stained-glass window fronts what would have been the off-licence bottle shop at the Fleet Street entrance, with the pub accessed from the narrow passage to the rear.

St Bride's Church is known as the church of journalists. From the presentation of one of the first printing presses by the suitably named Wynkyn de Worde in 1500 through to the last journalists leaving Fleet Street in the late 1980s, the church (and pub) has been their place of congregation, celebration and remembrance.

The final legend linked to the church is that of Mr Rich. Peering from his bakehouse window one morning, he was inspired by Wren's uniquely stepped steeple design to create the multi-tiered wedding cake that many enjoy to this day. The perfect pub in which to have your cake and eat it.

WHEN IN ROME: Take a tour of **St Bride's Church** itself, walking through the history of six churches, a Roman mosaic in the basement and a skeleton-stuffed charnel house.

NEARBY & NOTEWORTHY: **Ye Olde Cheshire Cheese, The Black Friar, The Tipperary, City of London Distillery**.

 Blackfriars

 95 Fleet Street, EC4Y 1DH

5

LEGENDARY LOCALS

'A good local pub has much in common
with a church, except that a pub is warmer,
and there's more conversation.'

William Blake

*T*hese pubs are not a destination full of glitz, glamour or literary heritage. Furthermore, your local is not closest to where you are, but closest to whom you are. These pubs offer subtle, understated charm where you least expect it, encapsulated by eccentric landlords and often long-time bar staff. There might be a platter of complimentary roast potatoes or a small finger buffet to dabble in on a Sunday, or perhaps a house pet profiling the comings and goings. These establishments add much value to the varied patchwork tapestry of our London villages, and the city really wouldn't be quite the same without them. Enter and enjoy their indefinable bonhomie, and just make sure you don't sit on the cat.

THE PRIDE OF SPITALFIELDS

BRICK LANE BOOZER

PATTERNED CARPET + NET CURTAINS + stove = a capsule of genuine old-school charm. Well-worn and homely. Perhaps the perfect East End pub?

Dating back to the era of Jack the Ripper, this unassuming no-frills backstreet boozer, with floral carpeted floor and a house cat named Lenny, changes very little as the world around it spins and morphs anew.

The area's industrial heritage, from the brewery up the road at Truman's to the local brickmaking industry, required a humble pub. Huguenot, Jewish and Muslim communities have made this area their home over the last 400 years, and the pub's name changed from the Romford Arms in the mid 1980s.

Local residents and a mix of younger, hipper patrons from the nearby worlds of fashion and tech add to the democratic jigsaw. The petite dimensions encourage the crowd to flow outside, and after a few real ales the spice pots of Brick Lane are just around the corner.

Get high-spirited enough and the piano beckons for a classic Chas & Dave-style East End singalong. With very reasonably priced offerings, it's easy to end up in suitable songbird state sooner rather than later.

In a world of filament light bulbs, hoppy craft beers, boutique gins and stripped floorboards, the Pride sails on without even blinking an eye or tipping its cap to such modern foibles. Bravo!

WHEN IN ROME: Take a trip back in time at **Dennis Severs' House**, described by David Hockney as 'one of the world's five greatest experiences'.

NEARBY & NOTEWORTHY: **The Ten Bells**, **The Golden Heart**.

 Liverpool Street & Aldgate East

 3 Heneage Street, E1 5LJ

STAR & GARTER

SOHO STALWART

THE PUB TAKES ITS name from the highest order of chivalry in the United Kingdom, although the current cohort of 24 Garter Knights and Ladies Companion might struggle to fit inside this inauspicious nugget in order to share a jar. A simple, uncluttered layout of burnished leather seating, etched glass, a few real ales and a cling-filmed ham or cheese roll for the peckish completes the picture. The poky nature of the room encourages a steady flow of patrons into street-side drinking, embellishing the classic summer Soho scene.

Beloved by the glitzy media crowd, who revel in the bohemian working men's charm, it's just far enough south of Oxford Street and northerly enough from Soho's centre that few tourists are lucky enough to stumble past this door. Wedged between award-winning restaurants, secret cocktail bars and private members' clubs, the Star has not swerved to accommodate any of these passing trends in its nearly 200 years.

On a street that was once inhabited by William Blake (note the upstairs bar) and Percy Bysshe Shelley, the pub and area were inspiration for Derek Raymond (aka Robin Cook, godfather of British 'noir' writing). His stratospheric fall from an Eton education to hard-quaffing Soho lowlife will unfold before you. Local chanteuse Elizabeth Billington's moniker as the 'Poland Street man-trap' simply adds to the street's rich tapestry of life.

WHEN IN ROME: Visit the **replica water pump**, remembering John Snow's discovery that cholera was a water-borne disease, and have a pint in the pub bearing his name even though he was a teetotaller.

NEARBY & NOTEWORTHY: **The John Snow** (see above), **The French House**, **The Coach & Horses**, **Dog & Duck**.

⊖ Oxford Circus

 62 Poland Street, Soho, W1F 7NX

THE CROSS KEYS

CORNUCOPIA

THE KEYS OF ST PETER guard the entrance to both the gates of heaven and this pub. To some people these equate to pretty much the same thing. This is a miracle bastion of boozing, a world away from prime retail Covent Garden.

During the summer months you ease your way past a curtain of horticultural bounty, and once inside it is forever 1975 . . . or maybe '65. Whatever the year, it is dark, red, warming, cosy – and just an utterly lovely place to sink some hoppy thirst-slakers.

It often feels like a brass band's instruments have been confiscated and stuck to the ceiling. The eclectic hoard of bric-a-brac includes a hankie signed by Elvis and a cricket bat from Sir Donald Bradman. A real treasure trove of peculiar ephemera and bygones.

The selection of Brodie's beers are often strong and hoppy, and it's good to see the offering coming from a reinvigorated East London brewer. The magic of the Cross Keys is that its patrons and paraphernalia make for an atmosphere that could almost be anywhere – that is, anywhere other than one street away from the buzzing and bustling West End. What a sanctuary.

For all the brass on show, the pub was in fact designed to service the nearby rookery of St Giles in the mid 19th century, to pacify and entertain the low-living locals. It now offers a simple refuge from the onslaught of modernity, retail and ever-rising commercial rents around the corner.

WHEN IN ROME: Visit the **Museum of Freemasonry** to uncover the intriguing world of funny handshakes and charitable acts.

NEARBY & NOTEWORTHY: **Lamb & Flag**, **Princess Louise**, **The Ship Tavern**.

 Covent Garden

 31 Endell St, Covent Garden, WC2H 9BA

125

THE WENLOCK ARMS

COMMUNITY SURVIVOR

A REMARKABLE PUB IN a quite unremarkable location. Originally serving as the tap room for the brewery next door, only the canal and converted warehouses nod to its industrial heritage. Passing canal workers and porters would have once provided fine regular custom for what is now a slightly out-of-the-way location, making this a destination pub for many.

With London pubs closing at a rate of up to one per week, how do you stop the torrent of burger bars, coffee shops and ravenous developers taking further hold? Answer: simply reposition the pub as the hub.

In 2010 the wrecking ball was aimed directly at this establishment, but enough community furore (there was a 'Save the Wenlock' campaign), coupled with the local council extending the conservation zone, saved it from demolition. Arrival on foot from almost any direction highlights the recent encircling of the pub by unscrupulous development.

The ensuing harmonious pub renovation revealed a 150-year-old mosaic sign, and the updating of the bathrooms can only be described as progress. Real ales, craft beers, ciders and Scotch eggs keep the locals sated and the Silicon Roundabout newcomers curious. The piano allows for weekly music, and the pub slowly evolves to suit the times without ever really failing to keep one foot in its glorious past. Dogs are welcome and there's an open fire too. What more do you need?

Even the rumour that it was once frequented by David Beckham and his grandfather should not dissuade you from a visit to this phoenix of beer.

WHEN IN ROME: Soak up the cutting-edge contemporary art at the **Victoria Miro Gallery**.

NEARBY & NOTEWORTHY: **The Eagle**, **Old Fountain**, **Narrowboat**, **The Charles Lamb**.

 Old Street

26 Wenlock Road, N1 7TA

THE COCKPIT

SHAKESPEARE WOZ 'ERE (KIND OF)

TUCKED NEATLY AWAY FROM major thorough-fares, this is a gem for those in the know or lucky enough to stumble upon it amongst the ancient alleys in the shadow of St Paul's.

The signage remembers its cockfight-ing history – before it was outlawed in the mid 19th century. Through curving glass doors, you enter into the sunken pit, with raised viewing galleries above from where people watched the bloodshed and en-sured the spoils from any bets. Legend has it that the owner of the losing bird would be slung into a bucket and hoisted into the centre of the room whilst other patrons let rip with glass bottles and bodily fluids.

Nowadays the carpeted floor, hang-ing whisky jugs and velour seating afford a warm and time-capsule welcome. A small selection of ales are dispensed by charming barkeepers, with a backdrop of banter from locals propping up the bar. A mixture of city workers and church con-gregants pop in here for a pint. With most pubs closed in the area at the weekend, the Cockpit continues to open seven days a week on these forgotten backstreets, offering the perfect hideaway for those in the know.

The blue plaque on Ireland Yard along-side the pub remembers the location where William Shakespeare bought his first house in London. He made his money outside the city walls at the Globe or Curtain theatres, but returned here to purchase a home within the gatehouse of the 13th-century Blackfriars monastery (see p. 91). He never actually lived in it, thus becoming an early buy-to-let investor over 400 years ago.

With the local real estate values being amongst the highest in the world, raise your glass to this steadfast, timeless boozer standing strong.

WHEN IN ROME: Walk to **Playhouse Yard** and remember the boozing Bard performing here from 1608.

NEARBY & NOTEWORTHY: **The Black Friar**, **Ye Olde Watling**, **The Viaduct Tavern**.

⊖   Blackfriars

   7 St Andrew's Hill, St Paul's, EC4V 5BY

THE PALM TREE

RED

NO MAN IS AN island, but this pub certainly is. Not many people just happen to be passing Mile End and the middle of nowhere, but a strange magnetic vortex sucks people through these pub doors. Approach from any angle and the buildings quickly fall away, leaving the Palm Tree marooned like a lone star.

East End pubs are legendary in style and these four walls tick most boxes. Survived the Blitz: tick. Industrial heritage courtesy of the canal: tick. Live music and the occasional singalong to entertain the masses: tick. Partitioned to allow locals their peace from the passing trade: tick. Dartboard: tick. Severe aversion to cocktails and non-alcoholic drinks: tick. An amalgam of distressed fixtures and fittings, and lighting so dim who knows what gin is on the optics? Tick. This place oozes redoubtable charm.

A down-at-heel, no-frills approach and a mixed repertoire of beers clearly has enduring allure. If Barbara Windsor wandered through the doors, no one would bat an eye. The rich cabaret-red drapes add a brothel-cum-Moulin Rouge flavour to events, suiting the live jazz sessions, with the scattergun décor of celebrity et al photos simply adding a certain louche *je ne sais quoi*.

Fair weather invites canal-side drinking, if imbibing in another century isn't quite your thing. Hang out long enough and you'll hear aquaphobic bar staff rebut a request for a glass of tap water.

The old-school cash register still rings out after all these years, and cash is unfashionably still king. Savour every second while you still can. Fashion and fads fade, but style truly is eternal here.

WHEN IN ROME: Hone your alpine skills at the nearby **climbing wall**, or stroll along the canal to the **Limehouse Basin**.

NEARBY & NOTEWORTHY: The Lord Tredegar, Morgan Arms.

 Mile End

 127 Grove Road, Bow, E3 5RP

THE TIPPERARY

IRISH

'Up to mighty London
Came an Irishman one day.
As the streets are paved with gold
Sure, everyone was gay,
Singing songs of Piccadilly,
Strand and Leicester Square,
Till Paddy got excited,
Then he shouted to them there...'

... IT'S A LONG WAY to Tipperary. It's a long way to go. It's also hard being a local pub in an area where no one lives. But for the thousands of young Irish soldiers who made London their home after WWI and found employment on the labour-intensive hot metal presses of Fleet Street, 'the Tip' eased many a homesick heart.

Originally known as the Boar's Head, it was renamed in the Irish soldiers' honour in 1919 and is known as one of the original Irish pubs outside of the Emerald Isle. Irish-themed bars now cover the globe for people in search of the craic, but come St Patrick's day in London this is the place to be. The original building is even said to have survived the Great Fire in 1666, being one of the few buildings in the city to have been made from stone (harvested from the local monastery).

A quaint shamrock-tiled floor leads to a dark, narrow bar replete with handsome etched-glass panels advertising the black stuff. Rightly so, for the Tip claims to be one of the first pubs outside of Ireland to ever pour a pint of Guinness.

WHEN IN ROME: Take a stroll down **Magpie Alley** and view the original crypt of the 13th-century Carmelite monastery, known as **Whitefriars**.

NEARBY & NOTEWORTHY: **Ye Olde Cheshire Cheese**, **The Old Bell Tavern**, **The Black Friar**.

 Blackfriars

 66 Fleet Street, Temple, EC4Y 1HT

132

THE GOLDEN HEART

SANDRA'S

IF WALLS COULD ONLY talk! These four would have enough fodder to fill an encyclopaedia or two . . . The pub has endured the rough, enjoyed the smooth, and still sails on in a sea of gentrification. Perched on the edge of Spitalfields Market, it used to serve the dockers, market porters and local bobbies on the beat.

Old-school landladies are a rare breed, but this pub is known as much for Sandra as for the pub offering itself. Born just around the corner, she bought this pub with her husband in the '70s and has made it an East End institution ever since. From opening at 6 a.m. to serve the market and brewery workers, watching the Irish and Jewish communities arrive, whilst becoming a fulcrum of the British art scene – she really has seen it all.

The closure of the market in 1991 saw the pub takings fall. The vacuum was filled by artists on the rise, including Gilbert & George first propping up the bar and still living around the corner, whilst the neon art and photos hint at a longstanding friendship with YBA and iconic bed-unmaker Tracey Emin. The bond is so strong between landlady and artist that they even own adjoining seaside flats.

Down below, the ghost of Elizabeth Fry – a Quaker prison reformer – is said to haunt the cellars to this day, watching over the pub. One suspects she might need to shuffle over and make some room down there for Sandra's ghost one day. It's hard to imagine her ever leaving.

The pub itself has a bare, understated vintage charm, with wood panelling, divided central bar, jukebox and the occasional artistic photo or artwork as embellishment. It gets absolutely rammed, so drinks are often taken kerbside. You might love it. You might hate it. But there's nowhere else quite like it.

WHEN IN ROME: Take a stroll on **Brick Lane** to soak up the street art, see the **Old Truman Brewery** and perhaps indulge in a famous salt beef bagel.

NEARBY & NOTEWORTHY: **The Pride of Spitalfields**, **The Ten Bells**, **Carpenters Arms**.

 Liverpool Street

 110 Commercial Street, E1 6LZ

6

TEMPLES
OF BEER

'Beer is proof that God loves us
and wants us to be happy.'

Anonymous

*A*ll good pubs should serve good beer to good people. But some just go that extra mile and focus a little harder on the wet stuff, with either a larger, more diverse or particularly discerning range. The burgeoning craft beer and microbrew industry has required a newer breed of pubs and bars to bring their products to market. Some of these are sitting on a fine line between pub and bar, but all are worth a visit in their own right – not just for the range and quality of beer but for a unique and noteworthy magic.

THE RAKE

PLACE OF PILGRIMAGE

A GEM. ONE OF London's smallest pubs delivers one of the biggest punches. The Rake was converted from a market caff into a global showroom for craft beers in 2006 by the Utobeer wholesalers based around the corner in the heart of Borough Market.

With over 100 beers available on keg, cask, bottle or can, it's no wonder brewers and ardent elbow-benders travel from around the world to drink here. You are as likely to taste something from Deptford as down under. The adjoining garden provides welcome refuge from the touristic hubbub of the market – and please don't try to sign the wall unless invited. You have to be a brewer to do so; it's their mecca.

In the shadow of Southwark Cathedral, it seems fitting that the brewing mortals are revered around here. Discerning drinkers travel here from around the world to worship at this utilitarian high altar of alcohol.

A vibe best encapsulated by the tab above the bar that simply reads, 'No crap on tap.' They really do live and die by the sword.

WHEN IN ROME: Browse the shelves of the Utobeer shop in the heart of **Borough Market**; or the more religiously inclined will enjoy a visit to **Southwark Cathedral** to hunt down a rare stained-glass window with a picture of a pub in it.

NEARBY & NOTEWORTHY: **The Market Porter, The George Inn, Royal Oak**.

 London Bridge

 14 Winchester Walk, SE1 9AG

THE MARKET PORTER

EARLY BIRD

WHAT MAKES A PUB an institution? A handsome prime corner site in London's premier food market? A starring role in *Harry Potter* movies? Rotating real ales and happy punters oozing onto the streets year-round? Welcome to the one and only Market Porter.

A pub so sturdy, so handsome in green-and-brick cladding and so perfectly poised on a sunny corner that you simply must pop in. The wooden floors are pleasingly robust and a central bar houses a range of 12 ales, and ciders, and there's pub grub waiting up the stairs.

Why not come for a working-day breakfast, when the pub opens early (around 6 a.m.) to cater to the remnants of the nocturnal wholesale trade in London's larder? Perfect for early birds, or night owls; it's not unheard of for City slickers to enjoy a morning sharpener here before plodding over London Bridge for another day of rat-race drudgery.

Pay homage to the thousands of porters that thronged London's markets and dock-sides as the empire grew and the Industrial Revolution gathered pace. Loading and unloading the cargo was thirsty work, so up to 2,000 calories a day were required from liquid refreshment to keep them going. The strong, rich, calorific and well-hopped stout was perfect fuel for the masses, and the benches outside the pubs were often reserved to keep the minions ticking over.

Commuters, tourists and gastronauts mix in this market institution. On a sunny day, join the throng packing the pub to the gunnels and drink up the atmosphere in one of the most ancient markets on the planet.

WHEN IN ROME: Don't miss a chilling visit to the **Cross Bones Graveyard**, where 'Winchester Geese' (prostitutes) found a resting place.

NEARBY & NOTEWORTHY: **The Rake**, **The George Inn**, **Royal Oak**.

 London Bridge

 9 Stoney Street, SE1 9AA

EUSTON TAP

DIMINUTIVE DORIC DRAUGHTHOUSE

'A Brobdingnagian absurdity'

Augustus Pugin

PUGIN OBVIOUSLY WASN'T A fan of the clumsy Doric arch that stood here from 1837, but we bet he'd love a drink in the Tap. It's a truly pioneering trailblazer in a quirky location, and is squeezing every grain of malt out of the small footprint to foist fine beer upon those in the know. Opened in 2010, at a time when the craft brewing resurgence was yet to take hold and cask ale was still largely unfashionable, the Euston Tap was a genuine game-changer.

The impractical size, cumbersome climb to the first floor and a beer garden so small that it redefines the genre mean you don't linger long. Hardly enough time to make a dent in the 40+ wall-mounted taps pouring a bewildering selection of both keg and cask beer from around the world, with accompanying fridges hosting yet more for takeaway or instant gratification. Options range from well-priced local casks to nose-bleedingly expensive and exotic imports.

History buffs revel in the Grecian-flavoured architecture and the two bars located in the lodges that once framed the famous Doric arch. Standing as a monument to the glory and glamour of the steam age, the arch was unceremoniously dumped in the River Lea. The underground tunnel linking the Tap to its sister operation across the road was even once used as a shooting range.

So whether arriving in or departing the Great Wen, we'll raise our wild, thrice-hopped sour to this historic and visionary hero!

WHEN IN ROME: Visit the **Wellcome Collection** for medical antiquities as well as cutting-edge exhibitions, or the **Petrie Museum** of Egyptian archaeology.

NEARBY & NOTEWORTHY: **Parcel Yard**, **The Queens Larder**.

 Euston

 190 Euston Road, NW1 2EF

THE HARP

CACOPHONY OF CASK

It isn't easy for the uninitiated to find a good pub in Covent Garden. The theatreland cash cows simply don't have to be top drawer to enjoy a heavy and regular footfall in this part of town.

Thus, to find the simple joy of the revered Harp a 30-second stroll from Charing Cross and Trafalgar Square makes it all the more rewarding. Other pubs seem to soak up the day-tripper piffle and the largely unexciting simple frontage is a masterclass in understatement.

Likewise, the narrow and plain interior hints at little out of the ordinary, but one look at the pump badges and you know that this diminutive building has a big heart full of beer. The passion for well-kept and well-served cask ales is what makes the pub stand out from the crowd. So simple. And so successful it was the first London pub to be named CAMRA's pub of the year, in 2011. Solid sustenance is found only in a sausage sarnie, and what excellent accompaniment to this repertoire of liquid finery it proves. No music, no TV, an upstairs escape from the throng, and even the sale of the pub to Fuller's by the long-term landlord Bridget Walsh seems not to have dampened the popularity of what amounts to a local pub in the heart of the West End.

Ebullient clientele often happily spill across to the sunny corner by the police station, or sneak out the back onto London's narrowest street for a crafty fag. Commuters, occasional lucky tourists and theatre buffs are all treated with the same chirpy welcome and united in their quest for a great pint and sausage sandwich. All hail to the ale!

WHEN IN ROME: Stroll down London's narrowest alley, **Brydges Place**, and maybe engage in witty chit-chat with Maggi Hambling's sculpture *A Conversation with Oscar Wilde*.

NEARBY & NOTEWORTHY: Lamb & Flag, **The Ship & Shovell**, **The Nell Gwynne**.

 Charing Cross & Covent Garden

 47 Chandos Place, WC2N 4HS

SICILIAN AVENUE

SICILIAN AVENUE

HOLBORN WHIPPET.
PUBLIC HOUSE V DINING

NEILL

HOLBORN WHIPPET

CRAFTY CORNER

THE WORD 'WHIPPET' DERIVES from a 17th-century term meaning to move briskly, with the dogs being one of the fastest-accelerating breeds in the world. An interesting fact, but still offering no obvious link to this pub other than whippets being lithe, good-looking and of quietly understated pedigree.

Sicilian Avenue has been offering its idiosyncratic, Italian colonnaded baroque charms for over 100 years. One expects chi-chi boutiques, gentleman tailors and purveyors of upmarket apparel; but alas, 'tis not as abundant as one might hope. The Whippet appears to have breathed new dynamic air into one of London's first and finest pedestrianised streets.

Away from the northern reaches of Covent Garden and without a tourist in sight, the patrons are a knowledgeable office crowd and beer pilgrims delighted to have such a charming outlet at their disposal.

It's an enticing draught-only situation here, so check the social media if you're planning a visit or gaze at the ubiquitous chalkboard to choose your poison. Narrow stools and tables allow for quite the crowd, whilst drinking on the marble alley is evocative of continental quaffing. Up to 16 choice serves are emitted directly from the brick wall, meaning one of Holborn's few independent pubs – and under the same ownership as the Euston Tap (p. 145) – has built up quite a following.

There's definitely life in this old dog yet.

WHEN IN ROME: Perfect for a pint after the **British Museum**, or seek out the **Novelty Automation** museum for something completely different.

NEARBY & NOTEWORTHY: **Princess Louise**, **The Ship Tavern**, **Cittie of Yorke**.

 Holborn

 25–29 Sicilian Avenue, WC1A 2QH

THE LYRIC

COSY CASKMASTER

IN WHAT COULD OTHERWISE be an unremarkable, cramped theatreland backstreet boozer, the strength of the Lyric's pump line-up seems to make all the difference.

The Lyric Theatre was completed in 1888 and is now the oldest on Shaftesbury Avenue. Its namesake pub has seen the great, the good and the not so good from the world of entertainment ever since. Actors and stagehands from the theatre, dancers of a slightly more exotic nature from the infamous Windmill club across the way, aspirant chanteurs and stand-ups on their way up . . . and on their way down. The old Red Lion pub (RIP) nearby on the corner of Archer Street was where Karl Marx and Friedrich Engels submitted their proposals for *The Communist Manifesto*.

On a street where a windmill stood until the 1690s, the plaque opposite the pub remembers the house of William Hunter, one of the pre-eminent anatomists and surgeons of the 18th century, who thrived on the abundance of body snatchers and possibly employed 'burking' – commissioning murders in order to acquire suitable specimens. Perhaps local hostelries like the Lyric provided a perfect hunting ground for likely cadavers ...?

An etched-glass and tiled entranceway leads to a dark-wood interior hosting up to 18 taps, and unfussy hearty fare in the room upstairs. Think of it as the Harp's (p. 147) Soho sister; simple and unabashed. Amongst all the associated bright-light madness, and only yards from the touristic black hole that is Piccadilly Circus, finding a good pub serving such a plethora of fine ales is truly worth singing for.

WHEN IN ROME: Bask in the neon erotic glory of the **Windmill Theatre**, London's equivalent to the Moulin Rouge, patronised by royals and a springboard for comedians including Bruce Forsyth, Peter Sellers and Spike Milligan.

NEARBY & NOTEWORTHY: **The French House**, **The Coach & Horses**, **Dog & Duck**.

 Piccadilly

 37 Great Windmill Street, Soho, W1D 7LT

7

INFAMOUS INNS

'Infamy! Infamy!
They've all got it in for me!'

Kenneth Williams

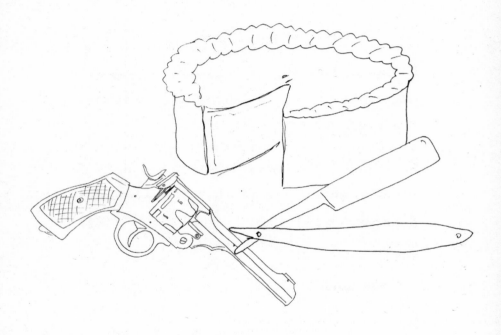

Everything very, very good or very, very bad has been plotted, schemed or has come to fruition in a London pub. This selection has been chosen for the events and people that have created an aura of legend and notoriety. They might be criminals, ghosts or serial killers propping up the bar, helping to stamp a place in history. These might not be the greatest pubs in London, but their reputation precedes them by such a distance that they are all worth a visit at least once in your life.

THE BLIND BEGGAR

THE KRAYS

THE MOST INFAMOUS OF them all. Forever linked to two notorious East End criminals and one brutal murder. A pub so capacious every London black cab driver was apparently in the pub at the time of the shooting!

George Cornell was nursing a pint in the saloon bar on 9th March 1966 when in walked opposing gangster Ronnie Kray. Maybe the beer got the better of George, who suggested Ronnie might be 'a big fat poof'. In no mood for banter, Ronnie calmly took out a Luger pistol and shot Cornell in the middle of the forehead as he rose from his bar stool. 'The Sun Ain't Gonna Shine Anymore' was playing on the jukebox. Either an act of strong territorial intent or schizophrenic instability. Possibly both.

The bar full of witnesses would never testify and it took three more years before Ronnie was charged with this murder. An ultimate paradox to this excessive violence is that William Booth delivered a sermon from the doorstep of the pub in 1865, leading to the inauguration of the Salvation Army.

Beer lovers will enjoy the pub's heritage dating to 1894 as the former tap for the Albion brewery, which produced the first modern brown ale in 1902, regarded as the 'sweetest beer in London'. England football captain and World Cup hero Bobby Moore even owned the pub, securing its East End legend.

The handsome building is worth a detour if you're in the area and the pub now hosts an open bar area, large beer garden, and simple, no-fuss charms. The bullet hole in the wall is long plastered over.

WHEN IN ROME: Visit the risk-taking **Whitechapel Gallery** where artists such as Picasso, Hockney and Rothko first premiered in London.

NEARBY & NOTEWORTHY: **Hoop & Grapes**, **The Pride of Spitalfields**.

 Whitechapel

 337 Whitechapel Road, E1 1BU

THE TEN BELLS

RIPPER HAUNT

EVEN SERIAL KILLERS GET thirsty. After a long night's work or whilst choosing the next victim, the Ten Bells would have provided a good hunting ground for Jack the Ripper.

This Victorian corner-boozer lay outside the secured walls of the City of London, in the midst of the sweatshops and slums of the east. Prostitutes, pimps and porters thronged the pub for alcoholic pleasures to help lessen the burden of life before retiring to their rented beds.

It's likely that the Ripper frequented the pub, possible that all his victims knew the pub, and that two of his victims – Annie Chapman and Mary Kelly – had their last drinks here. Mary Kelly's working patch was located directly outside, with her murder on 9th November 1888 ending the reign of terror.

Original tiled friezes depict the lives of the textile weavers of the day, with a more contemporary version showcasing the work of local artists Gilbert & George, who reside just around the corner. The pub balances old and new, mixing Victorian heritage with a modern twist for today's creative clientele. This includes craft beers, quirky cocktails and the occasional pop-up restaurant upstairs.

Jamie Oliver's great-great-grandfather was the landlord here during the 1880s, so he might have served the Ripper . . . or even been the killer. Unless, of course, the killer was in fact a woman? Or indeed Walter Sickert, Sir Arthur Conan Doyle or Lewis Carroll? Grab a drink, sit back and concoct your own 'whodunnit' conspiracy theory at your liquid leisure.

WHEN IN ROME: Visit **19 Princelet Street**, which houses the Museum of Immigration and Diversity.

NEARBY & NOTEWORTHY: **The Pride of Spitalfields**, **The Golden Heart**, **Carpenters Arms**.

⊖ Liverpool Street

▮ 84 Commercial Street, Spitalfields, E1 6LY

THE VIADUCT TAVERN

HAUNTED GIN GAOL

UNDER THE WATCHFUL EYE of Lady Justice perched upon the Old Bailey, the Viaduct is the last remaining Victorian gin palace in the Square Mile. A curving cornerstone in the heart of legal London, perfectly located opposite the old Newgate Prison.

The handsome façade invites you into a central bar purveying liquid pleasures to all comers, with a large block of ice being slowly chipped away for those with gin and tonic as their preference. Soaring columns, a Lincrusta ceiling, etched glass and mirrors complete the scene. A simple cash or card payment suffices now, but look to the rear of the pub and you'll see an architectural quirk in the form of an ornate wood-and-glass booth. Patrons would swap hard cash for tokens that could then be exchanged across the bar for booze. The risk of staff being less than trustworthy with cash was thus minimised.

The real *pièce de résistance* is the series of painted wall panels depicting agriculture, art, commerce and industry, mimicking the statues found on the actual Holborn Viaduct itself. Look closely and a bullet hole remembers an over-enthusiastic WWI soldier letting off an errant round, striking the derrière of one of the painted Victorian beauties.

For a subterranean adventure, ask nicely and you can often descend to the dank pub cellars. They might look like, smell like and have the atmosphere of prison cells, but alas, historically inclined pedants have poo-pooed such suggestions. All the same, liberal-minded fantasists or paranormal hunters might imagine inmates from Newgate Prison or the nearby debtors' prison residing down here in cramped conditions. Drink enough spirits upstairs and you might just start seeing them on a more regular basis.

WHEN IN ROME: Stroll across **Holborn Viaduct** to enjoy the architectural marvel, and legal eagles should not miss a visit to the public galleries at the **Old Bailey**.

NEARBY & NOTEWORTHY: **The Hand & Shears**, **The Cockpit**, **Ye Olde Mitre**.

 St Paul's

 126 Newgate Street, EC1A 7AA

THE STAR TAVERN

HIGH LIFE MEETS LOW LIFE

THE BELGRAVIA MEWS LOCATION keeps the worst of the riff-raff away; it's a classy place where the upwardly mobile brush up against the occupants of millionaires' row and those that serve them. A melting pot of toffs, celebs, debs, escorts and hangers-on. Back in the day, all were subjected to the machine-gun verbal abuse of the Irish landlord, Paddy Kennedy, who dispensed his tirades as liberally to the upper crust as to the lower slices. A democratically stellar night out was always guaranteed.

The pub's heyday during the '50s and swinging '60s saw celebrities such as Diana Dors and Peter O'Toole drinking here as often as they did at the smarter West End clubs. And whilst the West End darlings were quaffing champagne, the gentle-manly underworld came to the Star to celebrate a recent heist or plan the next. The celebrity patrons enjoying the frisson, perceived glamour and thrill of sharing a platform with known criminals.

Light-fingered locals included Peter Scott, who became famous for relieving Sophia Loren of a good thwack of her jewellery collection and then walking into the pub thumbing his recently acquired wad of fifties. Legend says he even stole a pair of her French knickers in the raid.

Most famously, it was in this drinking den that Bruce Reynolds and Buster Edwards plotted the Great Train Robbery. On 8th August 1963 they escaped with £2.6 million from a mail train, and their days of leisurely drinking were swapped for years of avoiding the long arm of the law.

WHEN IN ROME: Enjoy a quick circumnavigation of Thomas Cubitt's **Belgrave Square**, the most expensive square in the UK. Sheikhs, oligarchs and the elusive Barclay brothers reside here, but don't expect to see them down the pub.

NEARBY & NOTEWORTHY: The Grenadier, The Nags Head, The Antelope, The Horse & Groom.

 Knightsbridge

 6 Belgrave Mews West, Belgravia, SW1X 8HT

MORPETH ARMS

SPOOKY

THERE ARE NUMEROUS HAUNTED rooms, ghostly goings-on and ghoulish gas-lit stories entwined with the history of London pubs. However, only one has a 'ghostcam', and this is it.

In the days when Millbank was known more for its penitentiary (1816–1890) than its art museums, the pub was built for the prison warders to kick back after a hard day's shift.

Housing up to 1,000 inmates at a time, those convicts heading for Australia would be led to a subterranean tunnel, under the road and on to prison ships bound for the southern hemisphere. If someone was 'heading down under' it was a reference to the prison tunnel beneath the road, rather than the Antipodean paradise we associate the phrase with today. Even being a Pommy possibly comes from the acronym of being a Prisoner of Millbank (POM).

Today, a series of brick-vaulted cellars host the voices, moans and groans of the solitary-confined residents. A live CCTV feed onto the screen by the bar allows you to keep your eyes peeled for Aussie-bound apparitions whilst downing a pint or two.

Move upstairs to the Mata Hari-themed 'Spying Room', grab the binoculars and enjoy the view of MI6, home of James Bond and the spookiest building in London. With MI5 also just along the road, the Morpeth Arms is the perfect understated halfway house for a meeting of espionage minds. Le Carré, eat your heart out.

WHEN IN ROME: Soak up a Turner painting or two in **Tate Britain** and remember its former penitentiary past.

NEARBY & NOTEWORTHY: The Marquis of Granby, **The Speaker**, **Regency Cafe** (not a pub).

 Pimlico

 58 Millbank, Westminster, SW1P 4RW

THE COAL HOLE

HELLRAISER

'I often sit back and think, I wish I'd done that,
and find out later that I already have.'

Richard Harris

OFTEN DESCRIBED AS 'HALF-MAN, half-maniac', younger audiences were introduced to Richard Harris via his starring role as Dumbledore in the early *Harry Potter* films. A legendary hellraiser, in his later years he decided to take up residency in the Savoy Hotel. In 2002, his drinking exploits finally took their toll. An ambulance was called, and whilst being stretchered through the marble-clad lobby, Harris's final performance was to sit bolt upright and shout, 'It was the food! It was the food! Don't touch the food!'

Although he drank with Richard Burton, Peter O'Toole and Oliver Reed in his prime, whilst at the Savoy he eschewed the plush surroundings to nurse a bedtime pint of Guinness at the local pub. So the Coal Hole is now known as Richard Harris's last local.

Formerly called the Savoy Wine Lodge (note the entwined letters in the window), the neon-lit entrance and leaded windows give way to a dark-wood interior, long sweeping bar and various levels in which to tuck yourself away from passing tourists. An historic theatreland 'song-and-supper' club provided refuge here for husbands not allowed to sing in the bath, while Gilbert and Sullivan dropped in from the Savoy Theatre to steady first-night nerves.

Harris, when questioned by a policeman as to why he was lying drunk on the street, stated, 'The world is spinning, officer.' When asked how this was supposed to help, he suggested he was simply 'waiting for my house to go by'.

WHEN IN ROME: Quaff a cocktail in the **American Bar** at The Savoy, or see the only remaining authentic gaslight on **Carting (Farting) Lane**.

NEARBY & NOTEWORTHY: **The Nell Gwynne**, **The Harp**, **Lamb & Flag**, **The Ship & Shovell**.

 Charing Cross

 91–92 Strand, WC2R 0DW

THE GEORGE

CAVALIER

THIS HANDSOME BLACK AND white pub is often the first thing people see having won or lost their legal case in the imperious Royal Courts of Justice opposite. A pub in which to celebrate or commiserate with your counsel, depending on how your day in court has gone.

The traditional timber frame is a much later speculative wraparound (1898) of a former coffee house and hotel originally recorded here in 1723. A statue of Dr Johnson stands just across the way, and he is said to have used this location as his postal address.

Soaring eagles as well as legal eagles can be seen drinking here, with the Royal Air Force church of St Clement Danes sited on the traffic island outside. Bomb damage from WWII can still be seen to the rear of the church, and the famous bells of St Clement's still ring the nursery rhyme 'Oranges and Lemons' several times a day. Photos of bomber crews line the pub walls, and the pub itself took a direct hit early in 1941. The publican of the day gave the licence up with immediate effect.

With little explanation for the carvings of naked men chasing pigs and geese on the front windows, the main focus is a fine run of keg and cask offerings. The house ale, 'The Headless Cavalier', remembers numerous workmen and staff reporting a decapitated Civil War horseman smiling and laughing at them whilst riding off to the cellar.

WHEN IN ROME: Tea lovers should not miss a visit to **Twinings'** oldest shop next door, having steeped and served a nice cup of Rosie Lee on this site since 1706.

NEARBY & NOTEWORTHY: The Seven Stars, Edgar Wallace.

 Temple

 213 Strand, WC2R 1AP

THE MAGDALA

RUTH ELLIS

IN A LOVELY LEAFY situation just off Hampstead Heath, this pub's place in London notoriety dates back to Easter Sunday, 1955. A young model and night-club hostess, Ruth Ellis, surprised her lover David Blakely outside the pub, promptly shot him twice, and then continued to pump three more close-proximity rounds into him as he lay on the ground.

Ellis had been part of a love triangle between a former RAF pilot and a dashing racing driver (Blakely), and it's believed Blakely had recently punched her in the stomach to cause a miscarriage. Ellis took full responsibility for the cold-blooded murder, and in July 1955 she became the last female to be hanged in Britain. Her final words to the parents of her victim were, 'I have always loved your son, and I shall die still loving him.'

A crime of passion, and a possible mis-carriage of justice regarding the capital sentence. The public petition drew 50,000 signatures, and the outcry that surrounded this case is seen as being instrumental in the abolition of the death penalty ten years later.

Fans of the macabre can visit the spot of the killing, where an errant ricocheted bullet is said to have made a hole under the first window. Recent accounts suggest the landlord and a collection of well-lubricated patrons manufactured this with a hand drill during a late-night lock-in.

WHEN IN ROME: A yomp up **Parliament Hill**, to remember the legend that Guy Fawkes and Robert Catesby planned to retire here to watch the demise of government just over six miles away.

NEARBY & NOTEWORTHY: The Holly Bush, The Flask.

 Hampstead Heath

 2a South Hill Park, Hampstead, NW3 2SB

THE QUEEN VIC

SOAPER STAR

THERE IS SOME IRONY in the most famous pub in London being one that you can't even visit other than from the comfort of your armchair and via the associated idiot's lantern. Up to 30 million people tuned in to *EastEnders* during its 1980s heyday to see Angie Watts served with divorce papers. Even the iconic theme music with its cliff-hanger 'doof doof' is more widely recognised by the population than the national anthem.

A pub so dangerous that there have been five deaths or murders within its walls. Even after being burnt down, the Queen Vic (formerly the Balmoral) still retains its position as the fulcrum of Albert Square life. The long-standing brewery of Luxford & Copley appear to hand the keys out with almost wild abandon, whilst heritage fans will be aghast to remember Den Watts tearing down the division between the snug and public bar early in the series. The staircase is notoriously slippery, and every wedding, funeral, punch-up or business deal has its roots in the pub. It becomes an especially dangerous place around Christmas – and watch out for the ghost of Dirty Den buried in the cellar.

This is the archetypal London corner pub, built in Victoriana style with high ceilings, etched glass and wraparound bar, inspired by the now closed College Park Tavern on Harrow Road. Walford itself is an amalgamation of Walthamstow and Stratford, making the Queen Vic an assimilated idea of what a London pub could and indeed should be.

Today, art imitates life, with the now fashionable East End attracting developers wishing to polish up the Queen Vic. Sourdough pizzas, craft ales, cocktail caravans and filament light bulbs no doubt coming soon.

WHEN IN ROME: Go for a cuppa in **Ian's caff**, pick up a bargain on the market, or grab a snack at the chippie.

NEARBY & NOTEWORTHY: The Dagmar, **Pearls** and other reincarnations offer little formidable competition to **The Vic**.

 Walford East

 46 Albert Square, Walford, E20

8

THE MOST
EXCLUSIVE
PUB IN
LONDON

'Halt! Who goes there?'

An exclusive pub is an obvious oxymoron. Invented for the everyman, and the antithesis of the velvet-roped club, the true public house welcomes all comers. But in the heart of historic London lies a pub where mere mortals tread only upon invitation. A simple room where the classic pub sign hangs outside, leather banquettes line the interior, and a small selection of ales are available for consumption in memorabilia-festooned surroundings. Certainly more club than pub, it's an idiosyncratic hostelry so heavily centred in London's history that it features here for your own curious consumption.

THE KEYS

BEEFEATER BOOZER

THE TOWER OF LONDON is one of the capital's biggest tourist attractions, so it's easy to overlook the fact that over 30 families reside within its walls. The Yeoman Warders (known more commonly as the Beefeaters) have lived inside the Tower since 1485, looking after the Crown Jewels and prisoners ranging from the Krays to Hitler's right-hand man Rudolf Hess, and ensuring that the monarchy-saving ravens don't flee the nest for warmer climes.

Nowadays the Yeomen spend a lot of time narrating the Tower's epic history to visitors from far and wide, and performing the Ceremony of the Keys every night (hence the name). A timely tradition that has been going for over 700 years.

It's all quite thirsty work, and every community needs a place to kick back, share a drink and discuss life's finer details. Like villages across the country, this place has a pub as its hub.

Swirly-patterned carpets, pimpled leather chairs and memorabilia adorning the walls make it almost like any other boozer. Almost. The paraphernalia includes an executioner's axe and historic Yeoman Warder uniforms; the walls date back nearly a millennium; and the beer offering includes a quirky Yeoman 1485 and bespoke Beefeater Bitter. You can probably guess what brand of gin they serve, and they pop to the distillery across the river for Christmas lunch every year.

The pub has a rather exclusive door policy: Yeoman Warders and associated friends and family only. So there you have it. One of London's most visited buildings with a pub very few get to enjoy. If you are lucky enough to get the invite, remember not to ask for a beer with the head taken off.

WHEN IN ROME: Experience the ultimate lock-in by watching the oldest military ceremony in the world with the **Ceremony of the Keys**.

NEARBY & NOTEWORTHY: Princess of Prussia, **The Ship** (EC3).

 Tower Hill

 St Katharine's & Wapping, EC3N 4AB

9

THE
FALLEN

'When you have lost your inns,
drown your empty selves for you will
have lost the last of England.'

Hilaire Belloc

*L*ondon pubs might be revered the world over, but they appear to be a somewhat endangered species. Not quite rare enough for Sir David Attenborough to spearhead a conservation campaign, but the decline is certainly noteworthy and alarming.

Pubs continue to close at the rate of one a week, with the capital losing over 25% of its hostelries since the turn of the millennium. A truly parlous state. Devilish developers, rising rates and healthy-living fads have squeezed the pips on many an establishment. Changing social patterns, greater domestic comfort and of course recent pandemic pressures complete the economic pincer movement.

As an example, Oxford Street once boasted 38 pubs. Now there's only one – the Tottenham, dating back to 1892. This section offers a cautionary warning in the form of pubs already lost – the ones whose doors are forever closed. We honestly don't build them like we used to, so let's ensure there's always a good reason for a trip down the local.

CROCKER'S FOLLY

VICTORIAN MISFIRE

LOST AS A PUB but not gone forever, and still accessible if you enjoy your hummus as much as your hops.

Harking back to the speculative and moneyed Victorian era, the urban legend suggests that Frank Crocker heard that a new terminus for the Great Central Railway was to be established in St John's Wood. With rail travel being quite the thing, he thought building a splendiferous hotel nearby would be a total no-brainer. In order to attract the well-heeled travellers he spared no expense. He used over 50 types of marble, flamboyant crystal chandeliers, soaring marble columns and the innovative concept of a women-only bar. Hints of Versailles meet a classic gin-palace aesthetic reminiscent of the later work in the Black Friar (p. 91).

Unfortunately for Frank the railway never came to fruition in the locale, so the hotel festered slightly off-grid once complete in 1898. Struggling to find its place in the world, it was later often frequented by England cricketing legends from nearby Lord's, with Beefy, Gower and Lamby leading the crusade at a time when 12 pints of lager was simply de rigueur when relaxing after a long day at the crease.

Originally known as the Crown, the pub was renamed Crocker's Folly to remember the misplaced financial stake, and poor old Frank Crocker's ghost is said to haunt the premises to this day.

Beautifully renovated and reopened as a restaurant in 2014, it's well worth a visit to enjoy the palatial ambition and grandeur alone.

WHEN IN ROME: Follow the sound of leather on willow to visit **Lord's cricket ground** and its museum.

NEARBY & NOTEWORTHY: The Prince Alfred, **The Warrington**.

 St John's Wood

 24 Aberdeen Place, St John's Wood, NW8 8JR

THE TABARD INN

PILGRIM PUB

THE TABARD WAS THE famous starting point for Geoffrey Chaucer's 29 Kent-bound pilgrims in his 14th-century *Canterbury Tales* – often marking their first time away from the confines of the religious order. Finding themselves in the heart of the Southwark 'stews' (brothels), awash with 'Winchester geese', bawdy and humorous tales abound. The landlord of the pub himself joins the group to judge the quality of each forthcoming tale, and promises the prize of a fine dinner to the winning narrator.

Visitors to the George Inn (p. 17) can see a picture of the Tabard in the downstairs bar. And that's about as good as we've got to imagine what this rambling caravanserai-styled entrepôt of trade, debauchment and pilgrimage looked like.

The inn would have provided stables, board and lodging just to the south of the City of London. A place of loose laws lost in time to a large fire in 1676, with the later reincarnation pulled down in 1873 to make room for the burgeoning railway at London Bridge. The stagecoach era was coming to an end, and the requirements for such characterful offerings were simply no longer there.

All that remains is the works of Chaucer as the 'father of English literature' and his legacy being the first writer to be buried in Poets' Corner at Westminster Abbey.

WHEN IN ROME: Visit **Talbot Yard** to see the blue plaque commemorating the Tabard Inn, then pop for a pint at **The George Inn**.

NEARBY & NOTEWORTHY: **The George Inn**, **The Market Porter**, **The Rake**, **Royal Oak**.

London Bridge

Talbot Yard, Borough High Street, SE1 1NH

MOONEY'S

THE IRISH BAR

Stroll along the bustling Strand and stand opposite 395. Look down and you'll likely see a tourist tat-fest; but look up and you get some idea of the grand pub that once stood here.

The movement of Irish people to these shores has ebbed and flowed over time. Peaking in the 19th and 20th centuries as they fled the potato famine or joined in the post-war booms, it is often said that it was the Irish that built modern London. A rugby club bearing their name remains to this day, and their yearning for home and the craic can be seen and felt in the rich tapestry of pubs.

It's not difficult to imagine the long, panelled bar being thronged by those in search of hand-pumped Guinness with an oyster or two on the side. The barmen came directly from Dublin to ensure the finest pull, and the humble food offerings drew regular and repeat clientele. Patrons included commuters dashing across Waterloo Bridge, market porters from Covent Garden slaking their hard-won thirst, or journalists popping to Bush House or Savoy Hill for a BBC recording. Not forgetting those coming from or going to the many theatres hosting plays, ballets and operas in the area. Here are journalist Maurice Gorham's thoughts on what we've lost:

> 'It takes all sorts to make a world, and I have taken many a horse to water and found him too saucy to drink. But anybody who is interested in London pubs should not rest from searching until he has once leaned his elbows on the pink marble bar at Mooney's on The Strand.'

WHEN IN ROME: Head down Fleet Street to **The Tipperary** and remember it serving one of the first pints of Guinness outside of Ireland.

NEARBY & NOTEWORTHY: The Coal Hole, The Nell Gwynne, Lamb & Flag.

 Charing Cross

 395 Strand, WC2

ELEANOR BULL'S TAVERN

MARLOWE MURDER

THERE IS MUCH CONJECTURE as to whether it was actually a tavern, or simply a well-kept house down Deptford way. Either way, Eleanor Bull has become famous for owning the house in which esteemed word-smith Christopher Marlowe met his maker.

The date was 30th May 1593, and the 29-year-old Marlowe had been enjoying a day of feasting and boozing with a selection of men thought to be from the British intelligence service. Nobody enjoys that awkward moment when a bill is presented after a day's indulgence; unfortunately, receipt of the 'reckoning', as it was known, was too much to bear for Ingram Frizer, who stabbed Marlowe just over his right eye, killing the self-proclaimed atheist almost instantly.

Frizer escaped with a royal pardon, leading to claims of a state cover-up. Perhaps Marlowe was a man who knew too much . . .?

Marlowe himself, one of our greatest playwrights, ended up buried in an un-marked former plague pit just down the road within 48 hours. A strange and humble end for someone so revered.

But did he really die? Or was his death faked and did he move to Europe and pen the poems and plays later attributed to the one and only William Shakespeare . . .?

Where could such befuddled, gossipy murkiness occur but in a timeless London tavern?

WHEN IN ROME: Head to the church of **St Nicholas** and remember one of the greatest playwrights, buried in an unmarked grave right here after his untimely demise – a plaque on the wall being the only physical reminder.

NEARBY & NOTEWORTHY: **The Dog & Bell**.

 Deptford

 Deptford Strand, SE8

THE BEST PUB IN LONDON?

No self-respecting book on London pubs could be considered complete without referencing George Orwell's seminal article on the perfect pub. But rather than pluck or paraphrase, here it is in full unfettered format discussing the timeless pleasures of a cracking pub. The criteria applied are as remarkably relevant today as they were to a post-war clientele in 1946.

The Moon Under Water*
by George Orwell

MY FAVOURITE PUBLIC-HOUSE, the Moon Under Water, is only two minutes from a bus stop, but it is on a side-street, and drunks and rowdies never seem to find their way there, even on Saturday nights. Its clientele, though fairly large, consists mostly of 'regulars' who occupy the same chair every evening and go there for conversation as much as for the beer.

If you are asked why you favour a particular public-house, it would seem natural to put the beer first, but the thing that most appeals to me about the Moon Under Water is what people call its 'atmosphere'. To begin with, its whole architecture and fittings are uncompromisingly Victorian. It has no glass-topped tables or other modern miseries, and, on the other hand, no sham roof-beams, ingle-nooks or plastic panels masquerading as oak. The grained woodwork, the ornamental mirrors behind the bar, the cast-iron fireplaces, the florid ceiling stained dark yellow by tobacco-smoke, the stuffed bull's head over the mantelpiece – everything has the solid, comfortable ugliness of the nineteenth century.

In winter there is generally a good fire burning in at least two of the bars, and the Victorian lay-out of the place gives one plenty of elbow-room. There are a public bar, a saloon bar, a ladies' bar, a bottle-and-jug for those who are too bashful to buy their supper beer publicly, and, upstairs, a dining-room. Games are only played in the public, so that in the other bars you can walk about without constantly ducking to avoid flying darts. In the Moon Under Water it is always quiet enough to talk. The house possesses neither a radio nor a piano, and even on Christmas Eve and such occasions the singing that happens is of a decorous kind.

The barmaids know most of their customers by name, and take a personal interest in everyone. They are all middle-aged women – two of them have their hair dyed in quite surprising shades – and they call everyone 'dear,' irrespective of age or sex. ('Dear,' not 'Ducky': pubs where the barmaid calls you 'ducky' always have a disagreeable raffish atmosphere.) Unlike most pubs, the Moon Under Water sells tobacco as well as cigarettes, and it also sells aspirins and stamps, and is obliging about letting you use the telephone.

You cannot get dinner at the Moon Under Water, but there is always the snack counter where you can get liver-sausage sandwiches, mussels (a speciality of the house), cheese, pickles and those large biscuits with caraway seeds in them which only seem to exist in public-houses. Upstairs, six days a week, you can get a good, solid lunch – for example, a cut off the joint, two vegetables and boiled jam roll – for about three shillings. The special pleasure of this lunch is that you can have draught stout with it. I doubt whether as many as 10 per cent of London pubs serve draught stout, but the Moon Under Water is one of them. It is a soft, creamy sort of stout, and it goes better in a pewter pot. They are particular about their drinking vessels at the Moon Under Water, and never, for example, make the mistake of serving a pint of beer in a handleless glass. Apart from glass and pewter mugs, they have some of those pleasant strawberry-pink china ones which are now seldom seen in London. China mugs went out about 30 years ago, because most people like their drink to be transparent, but in my opinion beer tastes better out of china.

The great surprise of the Moon Under Water is its garden. You go through a narrow passage leading out of the saloon, and find yourself in a fairly large garden with plane trees, under which there are little green tables with iron chairs round them. Up at one end of the garden there are swings and a chute for the children. On summer evenings there are family parties, and you sit under the plane trees having beer or draught cider to the tune of delighted squeals from children going down the chute. The prams with the younger children are parked near the gate. Many as are the virtues of the Moon Under Water, I think that the garden is its best feature, because it allows whole families to go there instead of Mum having to stay at home and mind the baby while Dad goes out alone. And though, strictly speaking, they are only allowed in the garden, the children tend to seep into the pub and even to fetch drinks for their parents. This, I believe, is against the law, but it is a law that deserves to be broken, for it is the puritanical nonsense of excluding children – and therefore, to some extent, women – from pubs that has turned these places into mere boozing-shops instead of the family gathering-places that they ought to be.

The Moon Under Water is my ideal of what a pub should be – at any rate, in the London area. (The qualities one expects of a country pub are slightly different.) But now is the time to reveal something which the discerning and disillusioned reader will probably have guessed already. There is no such place as the Moon Under Water. That is to say, there may well be a pub of that name, but I don't know of it, nor do I know any pub with just that combination of qualities. I know pubs where the beer is good but you can't get meals, others where you can get meals but which are noisy and crowded, and others which are quiet but where the beer is generally sour. As for gardens, offhand I can only think of three London pubs that possess them. But, to be fair, I do know of a few pubs that almost come up to the Moon Under Water. I have mentioned above ten qualities that the perfect pub should have and I know one pub that has eight of them. Even there, however, there is no draught stout, and no china mugs.

And if anyone knows of a pub that has draught stout, open fires, cheap meals, a garden, motherly barmaids and no radio, I should be glad to hear of it, even though its name were something as prosaic as the Red Lion or the Railway Arms.

Evening Standard, 9th February 1946

* Not to be confused with the far from idyllic charms of the many homogenised Wetherspoon's outlets across the country using the same 'Moon Under Water' moniker. Yes, that was the sound of Orwell turning in his grave.

OLDEST, SMALLEST, REDDEST

OLDEST PUB
The Prospect of Whitby (probably)

SMALLEST PUB
The Rake

SMALLEST BAR
The Dove(s)

NARROWEST PUB (Zone 1–2)
Ye Olde Cock Tavern

TALLEST PUB
Faltering Fullback

LONGEST BAR
The Falcon (SW11)

REDDEST
The Palm Tree

HARDEST TO FIND
Ye Olde Mitre / The Grenadier

MOST IMPRESSIVE BATHROOMS
Gents: Princess Louise
Ladies: Knights Templar

MOST HAUNTED
Rising Sun, Morpeth Arms, The George
(on the Strand), The Viaduct Tavern

BEST SCOTCH EGG
Harwood Arms

MOST BIZARRE NAME
Old Dr Butler's Head

PUBS WITH PEWTER BARS
The Grenadier, Fox & Anchor,
The Prospect of Whitby

BARS DESIGNED BY MC ESCHER
The Falcon (SW11)

BEST GIN CABINET
The Ship Tavern

MOST EPHEMERA
The Cross Keys, The Nags Head, The
Churchill Arms

MOST DEAD PARROTS
Ye Olde Cheshire Cheese

MOST CHRISTMAS TREES
The Churchill Arms

BEST BITTERBALLEN
De Hems

PUBS WITH OYSTERS
The Cow, Wright Bros, The Guinea (Grill)

BEST PUBS FOR INSTAGRAM
The Churchill Arms, Crown & Anchor, Masons Arms, Sherlock Holmes, The Holly Bush, The Ship & Shovell

WORST PUBS FOR INSTAGRAM
The Nags Head, The French House

PUBS WITH FAMOUS ANIMALS
The Seven Stars, The Pride of Spitalfields

PUBS WITH FAMOUS LANDLORDS
The Guinea (Grill) (Oisin Rogers), The Seven Stars (Roxy Beaujolais), The Nags Head (Kevin Moran), The Golden Heart (Sandra Esquilant)

PUBS WITH FAMOUS OWNERS
The Grapes (Sir Ian McKellen), Fox & Pheasant (James Blunt), The Lore of The Land (Guy Ritchie and David Beckham)

PUBS WITH FIRES
Ye Olde Cheshire Cheese, The George Inn, The Seven Stars, The Spaniards Inn, The Holly Bush, The Flask, The Jerusalem Tavern, Southampton Arms, The Gun, Pineapple, Sir Richard Steele, The Wenlock Arms, The Grapes, The Pride of Spitalfields, The Mayflower, The Dove(s)

PUBS WITH MOBILE PHONE BANS
The Nags Head, The French House

PUBS IN THE MOVIES
The Globe (*Bridget Jones*), Royal Oak (*Lock, Stock and Two Smoking Barrels*), Turner's Old Star (*Legend*), Black Prince (*Kingsman*), Ye Olde Mitre (*Snatch*), Lamb Tavern (*Brannigan*), The Anchor (*Mission Impossible*), The Market Porter (*Harry Potter and the Prisoner of Azkaban*), The Black Friar (*Men In Black: International*)

PUBS WITH A BAN ON SWEARING
Any Samuel Smith establishment

PUBS ASSOCIATED WITH DICKENS
Pretty much all of them

**PUBS WHERE THE RULES OF
FOOTBALL STARTED**
Freemasons Arms

PUBS WITH ART DECO STYLING
The Peacock, The Duke

PUBS WITH TREES IN
Ye Olde Mitre, Waxy O'Connor's

PUBS WITH GREAT BEER GARDENS
Faltering Fullback, Crabtree,
Windsor Castle

FAMOUSLY DOG-FRIENDLY PUBS
The Spaniards Inn, The Queens Larder,
The Narrowboat, Hare & Billet, Red Lion &
Sun, Hand in Hand

PUBS WITH PIANOS
Southampton Arms, The Coach & Horses,
The Pride of Spitalfields, Anchor Tap, Lord
Clyde, The Palm Tree, The Nell Gwynne

PUBS WITH DARTBOARDS
The Champion, Bricklayers Arms,
Chandos, The Ship & Shovell, Lyceum,
Temple Brewhouse, The Angel, Anchor
Tap, Lord Clyde, Cittie of Yorke, Parcel
Yard, Rising Sun, Old Fountain, The
Wenlock Arms

NOTABLE FOOD
The Eagle, Harwood Arms, Anchor &
Hope, Marksman, Bull & Last, Old Red
Cow, Canton Arms, Drapers Arms

PUBS WITH THEATRES
King's Head, White Bear, Old Red Lion,
The Hope, Hen & Chickens, The Curtains
Up, Latchmere

TUBE STOPS NAMED AFTER PUBS
Royal Oak, Elephant & Castle, Swiss
Cottage, Angel, Manor House, Maida Vale

**FORMER FOOTBALL GROUNDS WITH A
PUB ON EACH CORNER**
Brentford (Griffin Park)

MOST EXCLUSIVE PUB IN LONDON
The Keys (Tower of London)

**PUBS WE'VE BEEN (POLITELY)
BARRED FROM**
The Seven Stars

**PUB MOST LIKE THE MOON UNDER
WATER**
The Lamb

WHAT'S IN A NAME?

With over 500 Red Lion pubs in the UK and over 20 in London alone, pub names often reveal their origins, reflecting ownership, patronage, geographic location, historical event, royal connection or sometimes just total whimsy. Here are some classics to add further detail to the pubs listed previously, and a few quirky gems to enjoy as you travel across the city and beyond.

ANGEL, THE
The angel of Annunciation...simple!

BLACK FRIAR, THE
Thameside 13th-century Dominican monastery

BLEEDING HEART TAVERN
Depiction of the heart of the Virgin Mary pierced by five swords...or possibly the murder of Lady Elizabeth Hatton

BLIND BEGGAR, THE
Tudor tale of aristocratic fall from grace by Henry de Montfort, blinded in battle and forced to beg at Bethnal Green crossroads

BLUE POSTS
Designated taxi ranks of the day for sedan-chair operators to ply their trade

CAPTAIN KIDD
Infamous privateer, buccaneer and pirate

CASE IS ALTERED, THE
A legal reference to a presentation of new evidence

CITTIE OF YORKE
Northern Roman walled town close to Samuel Smith's brewery, with old-world spelling for fun

COACH & HORSES, THE
Provider of services to those 'on the road' often dating to 18th century or earlier

COAL HOLE, THE
Historic coal hole, in this case for the Savoy Hotel

COCKPIT, THE
Bird-fighting bloodbath and gambling den

CROCKER'S FOLLY
Ill-advised businessman who created a white elephant in north-west London – or did he?

CROSS KEYS, THE
The symbol of St Peter at the gateway to heaven

DIRTY DICKS
Broken-hearted lover refused to clean anything or himself, becoming an attraction in his own right and providing onward inspiration for the eponymous pub

DOVE(S), THE
Symbolic bird(s)

EUSTON TAP
Referencing lineage to brewery heritage, and regional beers arriving into London through this portal

FITZROY TAVERN, THE
Named after the Fitzroy family, developers of local area

FOX & ANCHOR
With no obvious link to hunting or maritime pursuits, the fictional tale of a wily fox escaping aboard a ship for foreign fields is charming, whimsical and the likeliest explanation

FRENCH HOUSE, THE
Strong WWII links to the Free French Forces, Charles de Gaulle and all things Francophile

GEORGE INN, THE
Patron saint of England, and dragon slayer

GOLDEN HEART, THE
A metaphor for landlady Sandra?

GRAPES, THE
Botanical reference

GRENADIER, THE
Homage to the Grenadier Guards and their esteemed performance during the Battle of Waterloo

HAND & SHEARS, THE
Reference to the textile workers gathering here prior to the riotous opening of the Bartholomew Fair

HARP, THE
Musical and/or Celtic reference

HOLBORN WHIPPET
Fast-accelerating dog often used for hunting, fashionable amongst craft beer circles

HOLLY BUSH, THE
Fresh-cut holly was dangled across the door when the beer was fit for consumption

JAMAICA WINE HOUSE, THE
Remembering the West Indian traders who frequented the pub and locale

JERUSALEM TAVERN, THE
The Priory of St John of Jerusalem is just around the corner

KING'S HEAD, THE
Sign of royal allegiance, often replacing the Pope's Head after Henry VIII's break from Rome

LAMB, THE
Possible biblical Lamb of God link

LAMB & FLAG
Christ is depicted as the Lamb of God carrying a flag; also the symbol for St John the Baptist, with religious Crusader undertones

LYRIC, THE
Named after the nearby theatre

MAGDALA, THE
Home of Mary Magdalene

MARKET PORTER, THE
Named in honour of the hard-working porters who plied their trade in the London wholesale markets

MAYFLOWER, THE
Remembering the boat of the Pilgrim Fathers

MOONEY'S
Famous Dublin brewery with former presence in London pub real estate

MORPETH ARMS
Answers on a postcard please!

NAGS HEAD, THE
Bobbing lantern for pirate navigation, or more likely to reference a mews pub formerly housing horses and carriages

NELL GWYNNE, THE
Famous Drury Lane orange-seller, pioneering stage actress and notorious mistress of Charles II

OLD BANK OF ENGLAND, THE
The first law court branch for the 'Old Lady of Threadneedle Street'

OLD DR BUTLER'S HEAD
Charlatan purveyor of medicinal ales to cure gastric ailments distributed through a chain of eponymous taverns

ONLY RUNNING FOOTMEN
Former servants required to run in advance of carriages to clear the way of undesirables and pay any due tolls

PALM TREE, THE
Reference to former exotic canal-side wharves and their wares

PIG & WHISTLE
Possible reference to a drinking vessel (pig) and the call to wassail (whistle)

PINEAPPLE
Sign of generosity and hospitality, whilst also used as architectural motif after the restoration of the monarchy, with exotic fruits costing thousands of pounds

PRIDE OF SPITALFIELDS, THE
Named after historic local market

PRINCE ALFRED, THE
Second son of Queen Victoria

PRINCESS LOUISE
Fourth daughter of Queen Victoria

PROSPECT OF WHITBY, THE
Named after the coal steamer most regularly moored nearby, and easiest way to find the pub

QUEEN VIC, THE
Named after the iconic Queen Victoria

RAKE, THE
Hellraising, free-living flâneur and high-living playboy often with disastrous fall from grace (see Hogarth's work)

RED LION, THE
The most popular pub name in England, referencing heraldic emblem

ROSE & CROWN
Celebrating the end of the War of the Roses

ROYAL OAK
Tree used to hide the future Charles II from the Roundhead army following the Battle of Worcester in 1651

SEVEN STARS, THE
Likely reference to the seven provinces of the Netherlands and Dutch sailors as pub patrons, or alternatively a cluster of stars in the constellation of Taurus

SHIP & SHOVELL, THE
Named after Sir 'shipwreck' Cloudesley Shovell, Admiral of the Fleet

SPANIARDS INN, THE
Former quarrelling Spanish landlords, one who is alleged to be buried in the garden after a lost duel, a ghostly presence to this day

STAR TAVERN, THE
Celestial and religious links

STAR & GARTER
Insignia derived from the chivalrous Order of the Garter founded in 1348

TABARD INN, THE
Sleeveless tunic worn as outer dress in the days of Chaucer

TEN BELLS, THE
Local reference to the peal in Hawksmoor's towering Christ Church, Spitalfields next door

TRAFALGAR TAVERN
Commemorates the Battle of Trafalgar in 1805, and maritime links

TWO CHAIRMEN
A place for sedan-chair operators to pick up a fare, or refresh themselves between jobs

VIADUCT TAVERN, THE
Named after the eponymous architectural marvel spanning the River Fleet

WENLOCK ARMS, THE
Brewery tap for Wenlock brewery

WHEATSHEAF, THE
Nod to agricultural harvest, often found in country areas or markets (as is Plough)

WHITE HART
King Richard II's heraldic badge; this monarch first requested pubs to offer signage

YE OLDE CHESHIRE CHEESE
Most likely to remember the rarity of retailing the oldest cheese in England and onward consumption

YE OLDE MITRE
Named after the regular patrons (and their headwear) from the Bishop of Ely's palace next door

HISTORY
ON TAP

What's on offer behind the bar can often reveal as much history as the pub environs themselves. Here's our synopsis of the historic tipples to keep an eye out for and some of the more interestingly crafted options available to wet your whistle.

HISTORIC HEROES

Steeped in regional tradition, founded on ancient water sources, and often once supplying the British army on all fronts, their family names continue to underpin pub real estate across the capital, with their beer styles often now pivoting to appeal to the new generation of drinkers.

Adnams (1872)...Suffolk brewery famous for maritime-themed cask ales (Ghost Ship and Broadside) and a new boutique distilling arm

Beefeater (1872)...London's authentic London Dry Gin distillery still based in Vauxhall

Fuller's (1845)...home of London Pride, the iconic ale of London, with brewing roots dipped in the Thames at the historic Griffin brewery

Gordon's (1769)...gin of choice for 007, Ernest Hemingway and the Queen Mum. Old-school 'ice & a slice' classic.

Greene King (1799)...a once historic brewery, with family links to novelist Graham Greene, now trading as a balance-sheet-focused powerhouse

Guinness (1759)...globally famous Dublin brewery with its dark-stuff DNA soaked in London Porter, and a philanthropic legacy permeating London to this day

Hall & Woodhouse (1777)...England's second-oldest brewery, famous for Tangle Foot and Fursty Ferret ales under the Badger brand

Harvey's (1790)...legendary best bitter from the sweet heart of Sussex

Marston's (1834)...famous Burton brewer and purveyor of Pedigree, Bombardier and Wainwright ales to the masses

McMullen's (1827)...Hertfordshire heritage brewer and landlord of the Nags Head in Covent Garden that almost every London visitor has stumbled into at least once

Nicholson's (1840)...Maidenhead brewery opened by William Nicholson, who once paid for the pavilion at Lord's cricket ground. No longer brewing, but the name lingers on as a faux heritage pub brand.

Samuel Smith's (1758)...Yorkshire's oldest brewery, based in Tadcaster with an impressive London real estate comprising some of the finest historic pubs, all run in a traditional and often barebones idiosyncratic manner with no music, no TVs, no swearing and no digital devices

Shepherd Neame (1698)...Britain's oldest continually operating brewery, based on the North Kent coast with a cask range including Spitfire, once marketed with the slogan 'No Fokker comes close'

St Austell (1851)...Cornish brewer responsible for the easy-drinking Tribute and Proper Job ales

Theakston's (1827)...Yorkshire brewer of the infamous Old Peculier and source for the offshoot Black Sheep brewery in 1991

Timothy Taylor (1858)...home to a pint of 'Landlord'. A beer so well regarded people will even travel south of the river to sup this cult cask ale.

Wadworth (1875)...traditional Wiltshire brewery until recently replete with shire horses and coopers. Their top-selling 6X strong beer was first brewed in 1923.

Young's (1831)...brewed in Wandsworth at the Ram Brewery until 2006, now diluting their heritage by outsourcing all beer production, removing traditional pub signs and renaming their best bitter 'original' for reasons as yet unknown

THE YOUNG(ISH) PRETENDERS

Only born since the millennium. A fine selection of passionate home brewers finding a railway arch or other spot to indulge their career change. Experimental, innovative and collaborative by nature. They proffer small batch beers to the local area before branding it up, building it up and sometimes selling up.

Anspach & Hobday…home brewers turned pros, brewing porters and more in the heart of the Bermondsey beer mile

Beavertown…booming brewery famous for their quaffable 'Neck Oil IPA' with family links to Led Zeppelin

Black Sheep…Theakston's independent offshoot with its often revered best bitter or Riggwelter ales

Brewdog…much-hyped crowdfunding 'Punks' from a garage in Aberdeen to global domination

Brixton…local start-up referencing the history of the area with Electric IPAs, Windrush stouts and more

Camden…high-volume North London craft lager producer famous for its Hells variant and hard-to-hold widened pint glasses

Cloudwater…a world-renowned Manchester brewery with a tap room on the Bermondsey beer mile to enable the fresh sampling of their Double IPAs and other ethically crafted offerings

Dark Star…Brighton-based brewer with its flagship Hophead pale ale now found across the Fuller's pub portfolio

Four Pure…home to mass-market, easy-drinking citrus IPAs such as Easy Peeler or Juicebox, all squeezed out from their Bermondsey base

Kernel…the brewer's brewer and the stimulus for shaping London's craft beer scene. Fully flavoured bottled beers occasionally found on tap too if you're very lucky.

Meantime…still brewed in Greenwich but not quite as close to the meridian line as previously. It was an early mover and shaker in the premium craft lager market.

Redchurch…after its founder swapped a career in law for one in lager, this East End brewery is famous for its Shoreditch blonde that always goes down easily

Redemption…North London brewer often found on cask in the capital with a very sessionable 'Trinity' pale ale or Tottenham 'Hopspur' amongst the more regular options to appear

Sambrook's…Battersea brewer with some cracking cask ales including the Wandle and now resident at the historic Ram brewery

Sharp's…ubiquitous Cornish brewer of the thirst-slaking Doom Bar to be found almost everywhere as the highest-selling cask ale in the country

Sipsmith…tenacious Chiswick stillers responsible for the epic small-batch gin-aissance since 2008. Bravo!

Southwark Brewing…industry stalwarts keeping the cask tradition going in London's former brewing centre

St Peter's Brewery…Suffolk brewer known for their medicine-style bottled range and landlords of the wonderful Jerusalem Tavern (p. 63)

Thornbridge…regarded as one of the first craft breweries in Britain, with its signature American-hopped Jaipur making waves in 2005

Truman's. . .with heritage dating back to Brick Lane in 1666, the brand was reinvigorated in 2013. This eagle shall soar again. Yay!

Twickenham…one of London's oldest microbreweries founded in 2004 and famous for its Naked Ladies ale

Wild Card…a Walthamstow wonder driven by a trio from Nottingham and early mover on the Blackhorse Road brewery line-up

Windsor & Eton…founder member of the London Brewers' Alliance, their cask brews are perfect for a right royal knees-up

NO CIGAR

We couldn't publish an encyclopaedia, and certainly can't keep everyone happy with our selection. One person's pleasure is another's poison. So here's a panoply of great pubs, all considered for inclusion but which for one reason or another didn't quite make the grade. They might be temporarily resting on their laurels, chasing the less discerning tourist pound, veering towards gastropub status or hopefully in the process of making a phoenix-like return to top form. Pubs highlighted in **BOLD** are particularly noteworthy.

If you feel we've missed a classic boozer or two, then drop us a line at info@liquidhistory tours.com and we'll consider it for the next edition. There is of course no such thing as too much research.

Albert (SW1)
Urban architectural island

Anchor Bankside (SE1)
Pepys' Great Fire riverside
retreat

Anchor Tap (SE1)
Shad Thames Samuel
Smith's

Antelope (SW1)
Smart Belgravia boozer

Argyll Arms (W1)
Ornate gin palace in the
thick of the West End

Atlas (SW6)
Wood-panelled, ivy-clad
gem

Auld Shillelagh (N16)
East End Irish shindig

Barley Mow (W1)
Boxy

Bell & Crown (W4)
Homely Fuller's riverside
pub

Bleeding Heart Tavern
(EC1)
Gruesome Clerkenwell
corner pub

Blue Anchor (W6)
Hammersmith towpath
classic

Blythe Hill Tavern (SE23)
Catford CAMRA champion

Boleyn Tavern (E6)
Exquisite *fin de siècle*
Victorian interior

Bradley's Bar (W1)
Backstreet bodega keeping
the party alive

Bricklayers Arms, The
(SW15)
Local real ales champion

Buckingham Arms (SW1)
Politico Petty France pub

Carlton Tavern (NW6)
Risen from the rubble

Carpenters Arms (E2)
Pub bought for the Krays'
mother

Carpenters Arms (SW6)
Gastro corner classic

Cask & Glass (SW1)
Bijou Victoria quarter
gem

Champion (W1)
Sam Smith's stained-glass celebration

Charles Lamb (N1)
Islington Francophile

Chesham Arms (E9)
Phoenix

City Barge (W4)
On the Thames towpath

Clachan (W1)
Regent Street retreat

Coach & Horses (Bruton St W1)
Mock-Tudor vignette

Colton Arms (W14)
Brassy bijou gem

Counting House (EC3)
City banking hall

Cow (W2)
Gastro-Guinness and oysters

Crabtree (W6)
Relaxed Thameside beer garden

Crown (N1)
Barnsbury boozer (with snob screens!)

Crown (EC1)
Communist Clerkenwell corner classic

Crown & Anchor (SW9)
Bricky Brixton beer hero

Crown & Sugarloaf (EC4)
Sidestreet stalwart

De Hems (W1)
Pass the Dutchie on the left-hand side

Dean Swift (SE1)
Craft beer hideaway

Dirty Dicks (EC2)
Famously filthy classic

Dog & Bell (SE8)
Traditional Deptford welcome

Dog & Duck (W1)
Ornate Orwellian Soho boozer

Dove (E8)
Broadway Market Belgian brews

Duke of Cambridge (N1)
Trailblazing organic gastropub

Eagle, The (EC1)
Original gastropub

Ealing Park Tavern (W5)
Westy is besty Gothic gastro pub

Earl of Essex (N1)
Craft-focused Islington pub

East India Arms (EC3)
City brick bar

Edgar Wallace (WC2)
Literary-linked legal pub

Exmouth Arms (EC1)
Tiled market institution

Falcon (SW11)
Longest bar in London

Faltering Fullback (N4)
Towering, rambling and eclectic

Flask, The (NW3)
Lovely high-ceilinged stalwart

Flask, The (N6)
Stables, snugs and lovely garden

Fox & Hounds (SW1)
Chelsea charmer

Fox & Pheasant (SW10)
Heritage boozer

George & Vulture (EC3)
Dickensian chophouse

George Tavern (E1)
Historic creative hub

Gladstone Arms (SE1)
Musical Borough boozer

Globe Tavern (SE1)
Bridget Jones lives upstairs

Golden Eagle (W1)
Marylebone piano tickler

Gordon's (WC2)
London's oldest wine bar

Gun (E14)
Nelson's riverside love
nest

Gunmakers (EC1)
Clerkenwell cabin

Harlequin (EC1)
Sadler's Wells stage door

Hawley Arms (NW1)
Winehouse's winehouse

Hemingford Arms (N1)
Flower power

Heron (W2)
Home to the Handlebar
Club

Hole in the Wall (SE1)
Does what it says on the tin

Hoop & Grapes (EC3)
Great Fire survivor

Hop Pole (SW18)
Bijou Wandsworth wonder

Hope (EC1)
Smithfield stalwart

Horse & Groom (SW1)
Stable Belgravia classic

Iron Duke (W1)
Jaunty Mayfair watering
hole

Island Queen (N1)
Victorian local

Ivy House (SE15)
Local co-operative

Jack Straw's Castle (NW3)
Highest pub in London
(closed)

Jolly Butchers (N16)
Stokey stalwart

King Charles I (N1)
King's Cross charmbox

King's Arms (SE1)
Waterloo wonder

King's Head Theatre (N1)
Upstairs theatre

Lamb Tavern (EC3)
Leadenhall beauty

London Apprentice (TW7)
Isolated Isleworth charmer

Lord Clyde (SE1)
Tiled old-school local

Lord Tredegar (E3)
Bow beauty

Lore of the Land (W1)
Guy Ritchie's new gaff

Marksman (E2)
Hackney gastro giant

Marquis of Granby (W1)
Dylan Thomas and T. S.
Eliot haunt

Masons Arms (W1)
Floral Fitzrovia corner
classic

Museum Tavern (WC1)
Marxist museum piece

Newman Arms (W1)
The Truman show

Old Bank of England (EC4)
Grandiose banking hall

Old Fountain, Old Street (EC1)
Old Street freehouse

Old Red Cow (EC1)
Smithfield craft ales

Old Red Lion (EC1)
Old boozer and theatre

Old Ship (W6)
Another Thameside special

Pelton Arms (SE10)
Greenwich muso-local

Pillars of Hercules (W1)
Soho literary haunt

Pilot Inn (SE10)
Reinvented Greenwich
classic

Pineapple (NW5)
Kentish Town community
classic

Plumbers Arms (SW1)
Linked to Lord Lucan

Plume of Feathers (SE10)
Oldest pub in Greenwich

Prince of Wales (SE11)
Square pétanque player

Priory Arms (SW8)
Stockwell real ale
aficionado

Punch & Judy (WC2)
Covent Garden classic, *My
Fair Lady*

Punch Tavern (EC4)
That's the way to do it

Punchbowl (W1)
Guy Ritchie's old gaff

Queen's Head (WC1)
Charming King's Cross
local

**Red Lion (Duke of York St
SW1)**
Etched-glass gin palace

Rising Sun (EC1)
Haunted Cloth Fair classic

Roebuck (TW10)
Take the view

Roebuck (SE1)
Handsome Victorian
wedge

Royal Exchange (W2)
Paddington boozer

Royal Oak (SE1)
Harvey's London tap

Royal Oak (E2)
Flower market fulcrum

Royal Vauxhall Tavern
(SE11)
Iconic gay pub-cum-
cabaret

Salisbury (WC1)
West End gin palace

Sekforde, The (EC1)
Clerkenwell corner
charmer

Sherlock Holmes (WC2)
The drinking games are
afoot

Ship (SW18)
Riverside gastropub

Ship (EC3)
Hello sailor!

Ship (W1)
Fitzrovian freehouse

Simpson's Tavern (EC3)
Would sir care for a
sausage?

Sir Richard Steele (NW3)
Quirky Victorian
splendour

**Southampton Arms
(NW5)**
Ale, pie, cider

Speaker, The (SW1)
Parliament's weekday
local

Stags Head (N1)
Reinvented Truman classic

Stein's (TW10)
Germanic Thameside
biergarten

Swan (EC3)
Slim-line City slicker

Tabard (W4)
Theatrical tiled tavern

Tamesis Dock (SE1)
Floating Dutch barge

Tap on the Line (TW9)
Kew station bar

Temple Brew House (WC2)
Strand cellar microbrews

Toucan (W1D)
Soho Irish

———
BOLD: author's choice

Victoria (W2)
Posh Paddington pub

Victoria (SE1)
Charming Sarf London
boozer

Warrington (W9)
Ostentatious Maida Vale
hotel and bar

Warwick Castle (W9)
Mewsy Maida Vale

Westminster Arms (SW1)
Politico pint stop

White Cross (TW9)
High-tide washout

White Horse (SW6)
Beery Sloaney pony

White Swan (TW1)
Twickers Thameside
charmer

White Swan (TW9)
'The Moon Under Water'?

Wilton Music Hall (E1)
Quirky music hall

Windsor Castle (SW1)
Cathedral cracker

Windsor Castle (W8)
Panelled and gardened
wonder

Ye Olde Swiss Cottage
(NW3)
St Moritz in Swiss Cottage.
Bonkers.

Ye White Hart, Barnes
(SW13)
Barnes river boozer

Yorkshire Grey (W1)
Backstreet Beeb hideout

THE STOUT

REGISTERED · TRADE MARK

SOLD IN THIS ESTABLISHMENT IS OF THE

FINEST QUALITY ONLY

BREWED ~BY~ GUINNESS, SON & C⁰ DUBLIN ~FOR~

J.G. MOONEY & C⁰ LIMITED

GLOSSARY
OF TERMS

'D is for dull. To write dictionaries* is dull work.'

Samuel Johnson

*and glossaries

ABV...................... alcohol by volume
ALE....................... top fermented beer, traditionally unhopped, the king of pub drinks
ALE CONNOR........... professional tester of beer quality prior to public consumption
AMBER ALE.............. ale using amber malt to add red coppery tones and colouration
ART DECO............... bold decorative style predominant in the 1920s and '30s
ART NOUVEAU......... fluid natural decorative style predominant during 1890–1910
ARTS AND CRAFTS....... anti-industrial fine art movement from 1880 to 1920
ASSET OF COMMUNITY
VALUE (ACV)............ register offering additional protection from development to nominated
                       assets such as pubs
BARLEY WINE........... a beer with identity problems, brewed from grain, but classed as wine
                       due to ABV strength
BEER ENGINE............ machine used to pump beer from cellar cask to bar counter
BEERHOUSE.............. licensed house for consumption of beer on the premises
BILLIARDS................ traditional three-ball table game, not to be confused with snooker
BITTER.................... hopped pale ale
BLACK VELVET........... opulent drink of stout and champagne (Churchill was a fan)
BREWERY TAP........... local pub linked directly to nearby brewery
BREWPUB................ outlet retailing products brewed on site
BROWN ALE.............. originally brewed from brown malt
BURTON ON TRENT...... historic brewing centre famous for high sulfate levels in the local water
                       supply, ideal for brewing pale ales (see also 'GONE FOR A BURTON')
CAMRA.................... Campaign for Real Ale
CASK..................... round wooden barrel allowing secondary fermentation
CASK MARQUE.......... industry award for serving great-quality cask ale
CHASER.................. often small shot of low alcohol taken immediately after consumption of
                       strong liquor or vice versa

214

CHIPS.................... elongated fried potato, not to be confused with crisps

CIDER.................... alcoholic drink made from fermented apples

CIRCLE LINE............ epic yellow-line pub crawl including 27 stops...hic

CLOSING TIME.......... dispiriting end of an evening, typically around 11 p.m.

COACHING INN......... traditional hostelry with accommodation for the night suitable for travellers and their horses

COCKTAIL............... mixed drink containing spirits often served with spurious adornment

COOPER................. traditional wooden barrel-maker, a dying breed

CRAFT ALE/BEER........ brewer focused on small, traditional, independent methods and premium ingredients, often served at premium prices

CRISPS................... thin wafer-sliced potatoes, cooked and flavoured, not to be confused with chips. An ideal staple bar snack

DARTS.................... pub game using small flying arrows and circular wall-mounted board

DIMPLE.................. rarely seen old-school glass-handled tankard

DRAY..................... traditional side-less horsedrawn cart suitable for beer deliveries

DRINKING UP........... 10–20 minute window to finish glugging prior to closing

DUTCH COURAGE....... perceived bravery given by consumption of alcohol (Dutch gin or jenever) historically prior to naval battle

FREEHOUSE............. independently owned pub free from brewery tie

GIN...................... juniper-flavoured spirit

GIN LANE................ famous Hogarth painting depicting the many evils of gin consumption

GIN PALACE............. highly decorative gaudy pubs and bars from the 19th century

GOLDEN ALE............ pale hopped and golden-colour ale to tempt lager drinkers to the way of the light

GONE FOR A BURTON... slang term used for WWII Battle of Britain pilots who ended up in the drink (usually dead in the English Channel)

GREAT BEER FLOOD..... 1814 industrial spillage of over 1.5 million litres of beer in London, killing eight people

GROG.................... historic naval drink of water and rum, referencing grogram cloth worn by the vice admiral

GUEST ALE.............. beer offered in addition to any tied or preferred brewery supplier

GUT ROT................ euphemism for beer, associating the onward consumption with stomach illness

HAIR OF THE DOG....... superstitious use of animal hair in the open wound of a bite from the same dog, now referring to the additional consumption of alcohol to numb the pain of a hangover from previous consumption

HALF-PINT. . . . . standard unit of serving 284ml, historically only ordered when short of time or operating heavy machinery (e.g. automobile)

HEAD. . . . . the froth served on a beer, controlled by use of sparklers and/or type of beer, with northern areas historically preferring a larger creamy head, often to be disappointed by the lacklustre London servings

HOGARTH. . . . . great English painter, works including *Beer Street* and *Gin Lane*

HOP. . . . . flowers of *Humulus lupulus* used to flavour and stabilise beer

INN. . . . . a hostelry where a room can be taken for the night if required, often found on major thoroughfare

IPA. . . . . Indian pale ale, using hops to preserve and stabilise the produce for dispatch to the colonies

JENEVER. . . . . juniper-flavoured Dutch gin drink, precursor to all other gin styles

JUG & BOTTLE. . . . . pub with off-licence sales available, largely decimated by the growth of supermarkets

KEG. . . . . small beer barrel, often metal and used to serve lagers and craft beers under pressure

LAGER. . . . . historically cold bottom-fermented beer producing clear and mellow flavours

LAGER TOP. . . . . splash of lemonade or lime applied to a pint of lager

LAST ORDERS. . . . . final call to arms often signalled by a ringing bell to allow the ordering of one more drink prior to the bar closing

LOCAL. . . . . the closest pub to your place of work or home, or defined by the regularity with which it is frequented

LOCK-IN. . . . . Nirvana-like after-hours landlord invitation to continue drinking, with no sales of alcohol permissible, so they are complimentary or pre-paid prior to closing time

LONDON PRIDE. . . . . iconic London beer, named after the alpine plant that thrived in the bomb sites after the WWII Blitz

LOUNGE BAR. . . . . designated area with softly furnished seating, often carpeted floors and more expensive drinks (see 'SALOON BAR' and 'PUBLIC BAR')

MICROBREWERY. . . . . small brewery independent of major brewery or pub chain

MICROPUB. . . . . one-room freehouse, focusing on real ale, often in repurposed retail premises such as launderettes etc.

MILD. old-style often dark beer, enjoying sweet chocolate tones and with ABV around 3–4%

MILK STOUT. . . . . lactose-supplemented beer, adding sweetness and body

MIND YOUR P'S & Q'S. . . . be careful of your pints and quarts

GLOSSARY OF TERMS

MONOPOLY . . . . board-game inspiration for one hell of a London fancy-dress pub crawl

MOTHER'S RUIN . . . . term for gin due to its family-ruining propensities during the mid 18th century

NELSON'S BLOOD . . . . navy sailors' consumption of rum from a cask containing their dead admiral's body

NONIC . . . . glass with bulge near rim for better holding, stacking, cleaning and strength capabilities

OLD TOM . . . . a sweetened gin traditionally used to hide chemical impurities and poor-quality alcohol

ON THE WAGON . . . . attempted abstinence from alcohol, linked to signing a pledge of non-consumption or urban legend of allowing only one drink to the condemned man heading to meet his maker

ONE FOR THE ROAD . . . . . final drink imbibed prior to leaving the pub, with possible links to the condemned en route to the gallows

ONE OVER THE EIGHT . . . one drink too many, taking the consumer over the edge; suggesting eight glasses was the limit

OPTIC . . . . inverted non-drip spirit measure

PALE ALE . . . . light-coloured beer using predominantly pale malt

PASTRY/PIE LID . . . . officially **not** a pie, but thin pastry lid covering ceramic dish containing stewed meat and vegetables

PEWTER . . . . tin-based metal alloy that creates upmarket bar counters and tankards for the consumption of beer

PICCALILLI . . . . tangy vegetable relish with mustard, perfect in tandem with cold meats, pies and Scotch eggs etc.

PICKLED EGG . . . . hard-boiled egg preserved in brine or vinegar

PILSNER . . . . a blond lager taking its name from Pilsen in the Czech Republic

PINT . . . . standard unit of British alcohol equivalent to 568ml

PORK PIE . . . . cold meat pie encased within hot-water crust pastry

PORK SCRATCHING . . . . . fried pigskin, an ideal sodium-rich bar snack

PORT . . . . red fortified Portuguese wine, often served with dessert or cheese and beloved of gout sufferers everywhere

PORTER . . . . strong dark beer brewed from brown malt, named in the busy London markets and precursor to Guinness stout

PROHIBITION . . . . constitutional ban on alcohol in the US from 1920 to 1933, leading to the proliferation of speakeasy or blind pig bars

PUBCO . . . . a company that owns a chain of pubs, sometimes with brewery ties

PUBLIC BAR . . . . the least salubrious space to drink, but often the cheapest when divides remained, and perfect for a proletarian pint (see 'LOUNGE BAR' and 'SALOON BAR')

QUICK HALF . . . . code for 'I'd love another pint please!'

REAL ALE . . . . natural, unpasteurised, unrefrigerated cask-conditioned beer

SALOON BAR . . . . comfortable bar area, often with soft furnishings and premium-priced drinks, frequented by white-collar workers and their wives (see 'LOUNGE BAR' and 'PUBLIC BAR')

SAUSAGE ROLL . . . . meat croissant, served hot or cold

SCOTCH . . . . Scottish-made whisky aged for at least three years

SCOTCH EGG . . . . picnic staple of boiled egg encased in minced meat and breadcrumbs, possibly invented by Fortnum & Mason

SCRUMPY . . . . authentic unsophisticated apple cider made in the west of England

SESSION ALE . . . . refreshing, drinkable, easy-going ale designed for a lengthy knees-up

SHADES . . . . historic name for basement or cellar bar

SHANDY . . . . almost inexcusable addition of up to 50% volume of lemonade into a serving of lager or ale

SKITTLES . . . . table-top bar game where nine wooden skittles are struck by a swinging ball

SMALL BEER . . . . very weak beer, of so little consequence that Benjamin Franklin had it for breakfast

SMOKED BEER . . . . beer produced by drying malt over an open flame to impart flavour

SNOB SCREEN . . . . Victorian invention comprising mobile etched-glass window to allow privacy when desired from nearby members of staff and/or public (see the Lamb, p. 20 or the Prince Alfred, p. 108)

SNUG . . . . small private room frequented by the landlord's inner circle, or people of standing (priests, policemen, women) for whom a place in the public bar would be quite unbecoming

SOUR BEER . . . . intentionally acidic and sour-tasting notes as seen in lambic beers

SPARKLER . . . . beer pump nozzle to create additional froth in beer head, with divisive results amongst real-ale fans

SPEAKEASY . . . . secret bar found in the US during the Prohibition era

STOUT . . . . a strong dark beer created using roasted malt

TANKARD . . . . handled beer receptacle, sometimes with lid, and available in a variety of materials including wood, glass and pewter

TAP . . . . device for controlling flow rate of beer

GLOSSARY OF TERMS

TAPPING THE ADMIRAL .. the legend of sailors drinking rum from the keg containing the dead body of Lord Nelson, always said to have a very full-bodied flavour

TAVERN . . . . from the Latin *taberna*, historically linked to wine outlets but often synonymous with pubs in general

TEETOTALLER . . . . non-drinker of alcoholic beverages, derived from st...stuttering ab...stainer

TEMPERANCE . . . . abstinence from alcoholic consumption, often associated with a movement

THREE SHEETS TO THE WIND . . . . to be drunk, referencing the nautical phrase for loose ropes allowing a sail to flap, leading ships to flounce around like a drunken sailor

TIED HOUSE . . . . a pub obliged contractually to purchase all or at least some of its beer from a designated brewery

TIPPLE . . . . favoured alcoholic drink

TIPPLING HOUSE . . . . unlicensed houses offering after-hours drinking fun

TOBY JUG . . . . ceramic pottery drinking tankard modelled on recognisable figure

TOM & JERRY HOUSE . . . . beerhouses opened to stem the gin epidemic in the early 19th century

TONIC . . . . bitter-tasting carbonated quinine water, used to mix with gin and offering mild prophylactic against malaria

ULLAGE . . . . the accidental loss of alcoholic liquid in drip trays etc.

WET LED . . . . drinking-focused pub, often in decline due to the move towards family-friendly food-led pubs, but often seen as the bastion of traditional boozing

WHEAT BEER . . . . wheat-dominated brew producing often-hazy pints, and even hazier hangovers

WHISKY . . . . strong alcoholic spirit from mashed grain, with every Scotch being a whisky, but not every whisky being Scotch

WIFE BEATER . . . . archaic un-PC synonym for mass-produced, widely distributed cheap, strong lager with associated violent behavioural issues – e.g. Stella Artois (see also ill-fitting singlets associated with drinkers of the same)

WILD BEER . . . . beer produced using Brettanomyces fungus yeast. Yum!

WINE . . . . alcoholic drink derived from fermented grapes

YARD OF ALE . . . . long bulbous glass often used by alpha-males to drink 2.5 pints in competition conditions, with the world record being under five seconds

YOUR ROUND . . . . the unshirkable duty of buying reciprocal drinks for those in your party

PUBS BY TUBE STOP

Our choice of the top taverns closest to every Tube station in Zones 1 & 2 perfectly placed for an easy meet, greet and eat. Pubs with full printed entry featured in **BOLD**.

ALDGATE..................... Hoop & Grapes

ALDGATE EAST............... Hoop & Grapes

ANGEL......................The Charles Lamb

BAKER STREET.....................Barley Mow

BANK & MONUMENT
..............**The Jamaica Wine House (p. 74)**

BARBICAN........The Hand & Shears (p. 70)

BAYSWATER.... The Churchill Arms* (p. 102)

BERMONDSEY.............The Angel (p. 53)

BLACKFRIARS.........The Black Friar (p. 91)

BOND STREET...................The Iron Duke

BOROUGH .... Royal Oak

CANARY WHARF..........The Grapes (p. 44)

CANNON STREET.....................The Bell

CHANCERY LANE....Cittie of Yorke (p. 105)

CHARING CROSS..........The Harp (p. 147)

COVENT GARDEN....... Lamb & Flag (p. 25)

EARLS COURT....................Hansom Cab

EDGWARE ROAD..................The Victoria

ELEPHANT & CASTLE............Albert Arms

EMBANKMENT... The Ship & Shovell (p. 101)

EUSTON SQUARE....... Euston Tap (p. 145)

FARRINGDON
.................**The Jerusalem Tavern (p. 63)**

FENCHURCH STREET......... East India Arms

GLOUCESTER ROAD......... Anglesea Arms*

GOODGE STREET
.....................**The Fitzroy Tavern (p. 28)**

GREAT PORTLAND STREET....Masons Arms*

GREENWICH DLR...Trafalgar Tavern (p. 48)

GREEN PARK.......The Guinea (Grill) (p. 78)

HAMMERSMITH...........The Dove(s) (p. 39)

HAMPSTEAD.......The Spaniards Inn (p. 22)

HIGH STREET
KENSINGTON............The Windsor Castle

HOLBORN ....The Ship Tavern (p. 80)

HYDE PARK CORNER
.....................**The Grenadier (p. 66)**

KING'S CROSS
ST PANCRAS ....Sir John Betjeman

KING'S CROSS..................King Charles I

KNIGHTSBRIDGE......The Nags Head (p. 69)

LAMBETH NORTH........... The Three Stags

◉ LANCASTER GATE.................The Mitre

◉ LEICESTER SQUARE............The Salisbury

◉ LIVERPOOL STREET...............Dirty Dicks

◉ **LONDON BRIDGE.....The George Inn (p. 17)**

◉ **MANSION HOUSE...Ye Olde Watling (p. 111)**

◉ MARBLE ARCH..............Carpenters Arms

◉ MARYLEBONE.................Take a hip flask

◉ **MILE END............. The Palm Tree (p. 131)**

◉ MOORGATE..............Old Dr Butler's Head

◉ **NOTTING HILL GATE**
................**The Churchill Arms (p.102)**

◉ OLD STREET.................The Old Fountain

◉ OXFORD CIRCUS.................Argyll Arms

◉ PADDINGTON.....................The Victoria

◉ **PICCADILLY CIRCUS.......The Lyric (p. 150)**

◉ PIMLICO...................................Cask

◉ **QUEENSWAY...The Churchill Arms* (p. 102)**

◉ REGENT'S PARK.............The Masons Arms

◉ **ROTHERHITHE**
(Overground).........The Mayflower (p. 47)

◉ **RUSSELL SQUARE**
The Queens Larder (p. 85)/The Lamb (p. 20)

◉ SLOANE SQUARE...............The Antelope

◉ SOUTH KENSINGTON........ Anglesea Arms

◉ SOUTHWARK.........................The Ring

◉ ST JAMES PARK.............Buckingham Arms

◉ **ST JOHN'S WOOD...Crocker's Folly (p. 185)**

◉ **ST PAUL'S........The Viaduct Tavern (p. 161)**

◉ TEMPLE........................ Edgar Wallace

◉ **TOTTENHAM COURT ROAD**
....................**The Fitzroy Tavern (p. 28)**

◉ TOWER HILL...............Princess of Prussia

◉ VAUXHALL....................The Royal Oak

◉ VICTORIA....................... Cask & Glass

◉ WALFORD EAST...............The Queen Vic

◉ **WAPPING....The Prospect of Whitby (p. 43)**

◉ WARREN STREET........The Lore of the Land*

◉ **WARWICK AVENUE**
....................**The Prince Alfred (p. 108)**

◉ WATERLOO........................King's Arms

◉ WESTMINSTER...........St Stephen's Tavern

◉ **WHITECHAPEL.....The Blind Beggar (p. 156)**

_____

*10 min walk or more.

PATRONS OF PUBS

The names listed below are all fine patrons of pubs we've shared a drink or five with on our trundles over the years and who pledged their support to help make this book happen. We thank you and raise a glass to your good health.

1. ALEXANDER LARHAM
2. KAREN WELMAN
3. KAT DAVIS
4. JON VALLANCE
5. HENRY VINES
6. JAMES WILLS
7. PHILIP WARLAND
8. ERIN GREEN
9. DARREN STOBBART
10. PATRICIA DE JONG
11. GEORGE GINGELL
12. DAVID MCGRATH
13. DAVE WILGROVE
14. NEV & GILL LEANING
15. DAN GRIFFITH
16. CHRISTINA BIRTLES
17. JOHN G. STEPHEN
18. JEFF BARLEY
19. DAVID BASSETT
20. MICHAEL ROBINSON
21. A Q KOPP
22. WANDA PIONTEK
23. SIMON WINFIELD
24. LUCY EATES
25. STUART GUEST-SMITH
26. ADAM KINSMAN
27. ANDREW LOWE
28. DANIEL & ALISON HOOKEY
29. MARK HITCHINS
30. SIMON WATERFALL
31. RANDY WOOD
32. ADRIAN BABER
33. JOHN POLLACK
34. DAVID & JAMES COWLES
35. JOHN DOWNS
36. RON BONHAM
37. TIM MILES
38. FRANCES DOWNEY
39. RUSSELL & LYDIA PERSKY
40. DANIEL & AISLYN SCHOLEY
41. MICHAEL & SHARON SCHOLEY
42. LESLIE VINCENT
43. JOHN RILEY
44. DAVID EDGE
45. SHONDA SCHAEFER
46. SHANNON DEVEGA
47. LORI STEVENS
48. DENISE ROBERSON
49. CATHY PEREZ
50. MONICA DUFF

51.	CHERYL MATHISON	76.	CHRIS & KATE SKAE
52.	DAWN BUSCHER	77.	TRACY PURCHES
53.	JOANN JORDAN	78.	MICHAEL WINTERFLOOD
54.	CHRIS THORMAN	79.	MICHELE & JAMIE
55.	RICHARD P CASTAGNA JR	80.	NAN & LARA
56.	THOMAS BURRELL	81.	JACK ORRELLS
57.	ALEC CORMACK	82.	JAYNE STREAK
58.	BARBARA STOCKBERGER	83.	DEBBIE POWELL
59.	LAURENCE O'GRADY	84.	SPENCER DOODSON
60.	MARTIN HOLLANDS	85.	JAMES MOULD
61.	KELLY HAYDT	86.	TRUDE SCOTT
62.	KYLE & SARA BALUM	87.	TODD RUBRIGHT
63.	MATT WRAY	88.	IAN LATIMER
64.	PAUL FRENCH	89.	STEPHEN MEADOWS
65.	SHERILL CHAPMAN	90.	JOHN FREEMAN
66.	JAMES ROBERTS	91.	MATTHEW AND SARA PETERSON
67.	ANDREW CARTER	92.	DARREN VURNUM
68.	PETER NEWMAN	93.	HOLLY LOSE
69.	TANYA LAGE	94.	JEFFREY CONNER
70.	STEVE LAGE	95.	ANDREA MCFADDEN
71.	ALEXIS HOOD	96.	EDD CHARNLEY
72.	CHRIS NOTTAGE	97.	SIMON HOGARTH
73.	DAVE BURT	98.	PATRICIA HILL
74.	DEREK & ELLEN NORDGREN	99.	LINTON BRETTLE
75.	PHIL DACK	100.	KELLY FAHEY

PUB INDEX

Tick-box challenge included for competitive elbow-bending.

224

PUB INDEX

* Closed or fictional

ABOUT THE AUTHOR

After studying for a finance degree in the City of London, John Warland moved into garden design, winning six RHS Gold medals and tinkering in the Queen's backyard at Windsor Castle along the way.

With green-fingered pastimes being rather thirsty work, a passion for characterful watering holes led John to make a career out of going to the pub, establishing Liquid History Tours in 2011. Now easing into his forties and based in Richmond, he spends his time exploring the streets of London and beyond in search of quirky history, liquid refreshment and of course his very own 'Moon Under Water'.